PSYCHOLOGY IN MAN

What It Means To Have The Mind Of Christ

L. B.
RODRIGUEZ

WILSON
W L
LEGACY
Publishers

Copyright © 2019 by L. B. Rodriguez
www.lbrodriguez.com

Published by Wilson Legacy Publishers
www.howmayihelpyou.com

Book Cover Artwork by Eliezer Pagan
Book Design by How May I Help You
ISBN-13: 978-1-7344029-0-2
Printed in the United States of America

DEDICATION

I dedicate this book to the memory of my mother. She had no official schooling, but she showed us that education starts at home, putting God first in everything we do. She taught us humility and respect for others. She shared a lot of her wisdom, which I know today was the Lord's revelation of wisdom that is so very different from what the world tells us. She had an amazing motherly instinct that allowed her to know when we were hurt or in trouble. She never complained about being too tired to make us something to eat. I never realized how poor we were growing up because when we were hungry, she was always able to make something out of nothing. I am blessed to have that trait today also, creating meals with whatever I find in the pantry and fridge. My mother told me at an early age that many would not understand me, but that was okay because people did much more to Jesus and He overcame it all for the Father's glory.

Thank you, Mommy!

CONTENTS

FORWARD

A s you read this book, you will learn the life of a humble woman, who has gone from one hardship to another, walking in faith. It is her story explained in a simple manner that will inspire you. Being able to open and share our lives with others, putting ourselves out there, is a challenging task for many. Yet, as you will see, she does a marvelous job in doing so. She does not seek pity or glory, instead she just wants to share her life's toughest times and how her faith saved her. It is in the trivial things that she can move on and even show us how to overcome our own mishaps that happen in all our lives.

In her story, she drives us to truly be clear on what we want. It is a crucial element in living our lives with intention. She speaks on how we must learn to be active in our lives and be able to create for ourselves that which we may want. Just like L. B. Rodriguez, came into my life one day as a participant of one of my trainings, I knew then as I do now, that there is always something, we are to learn from everyone, even if we do not see it then.

Her book will touch your soul and heart by opening your eyes to simple things around your lives. As she herself says many times, "Whether we want to admit it or not we are all connected and in one way or another bring something to the table."

Maggie C. Lopez. PhD

T oday, as never before, people of God are interested in learning how psychology will help them and what it has to say about mankind. The study of Psychology from a Spiritual Perspective in Man deals with the mindset of man, and of the author L. B. Rodriguez's extraordinary testimony and journey to find the truth of the Gospel of Jesus Christ has inspired many, including her family members, and friends. L. B. Rodriguez expresses on how the four sets of emotions common to all—helps us to accept by faith the principles in God's Word or reject them. As we read Psychology in Man, we can see how the four sets of emotions are addressed in her own life.

L. B. Rodriguez had to travel over many hurdles in her journey, showing her four sets of emotion. By reading closely, you will first encounter how L. B. Rodriguez faces fear-anxiety-apprehension syndrome in the mist of what she had to endure as a single Mom and the sense of loss. "There were moments of no help for mankind." Psychology in Man approaches by life experiences that this plague can hit us too; unless we get relief from them, they will ultimately destroy us. With this in mind, L. B. Rodriguez begins sharing her journey to find the truth of the Word of God in reaching out on How to have the Mindset of Christ.

The second set of emotions that bothers us is the anger-hostility-hated syndrome. As to why did this happen to me? Why me God? This is a question that everyone asks when we are going through difficult moments of desperation. The sense of feeling loss, when one feels that the world cares nothing for the individual who has apparently violated religious rites in the Roman Catholic Church. Christ died for our sins, as the scriptures read in

Romans 3:23 – "...for all have sinned and fall short of the glory of God." Salvation is instantaneous, and holiness is progressive, as we come to Christ we are constantly working on "Being Holy, as He is Holy". God is working in our lives constantly. If we have confessed that Jesus Christ is Lord, then what the Lord has clean, let no man say is common. As in Act 10:15. which says, "But the voice spoke from heaven a second time, 'Do not call anything impure that God has made clean'". God the Son Jesus died on the cross of Calvary and died for our sins. Who are we to go to the depths of the sea, to dig out sins that God the Son Jesus has forgiven us? As quoted in the Book of Micah 7:19, "He will turn again, he will have compassion upon us; he will subdue our iniquities; and thou wilt cast all their sins into the depths of the sea. Now my question is: to have the mindset of Jesus, do we go back to the deep part of the sea to fish out our forgiven sins? No, way we do not go back!

L. B. Rodriguez faces the third set of emotions that we are plagued with which is that of the depression-guilt-psychic pain syndrome. The majority of people that occupy hospital beds are there not because of physical illness, but because of emotional, mental, and psychological problems. The enemy will play with our mindset to have us believe that we are failures because we did not meet the expectation of mankind secular and religious mind and set of rules. But we have been redeemed by the Blood of the Lamb, we have the mind of Christ, the need to feel depressed is real and the guilt is real as well. These feelings are present but know that the enemy plays with our minds to make us feel a sense of hopelessness. Abiding sorrow that bothers every individual is real. But the Holy Spirit comes to our refuge, if we allow Him too.

He is the Third Person of the Trinity, God the Father, God the Son Jesus, and God the Holy Spirit. When we yield, give our life to our Lord and Savior, and submit our will to God, the Holy Spirit will come to abide in us. L. B. Rodriguez experiences the move of the Holy Spirit in her life. A life of transformation from fear-anxiety-apprehension, anger-hostility-hated, depression-guilt and pain. All these feelings are for real, but the Holy Spirit is just as real, and His job is to fill all these voids that L. B. Rodriguez yearns and seeks out for in her life. She found the Lord of Peace. She found abundance of life and purpose. She found the peace of God that surpassed all of our own understanding.

The fourth and last set of emotions that L. B. Rodriguez had to conquer through Christ Jesus was the mindset of a conqueror. The fourth emotion that bothers us is what may be termed as destructive egotism, which is another form of fear. "I am myself, I have an ego, and I have desire to have it built up to a certain degree. And yet in my desires to have my ego built up, there is a certain amount of fear, and so I am trying to balance my fears with my ego as an individual, and this is an area that gives everyone problems. L. B. Rodriguez battles against opposition within her family and church, in trying to build her ego, instead she got hurt again and again from love ones that were there to protect her and nurture her spiritually and instead condemned her in ways that did not allow her to reach fullness of joy and peace in trying to strive in life despite of her life driven purpose.

Over against these four sets of adverse emotions, L. B. Rodriguez is able to conquer through the work of the Holy Spirit and learning to live by the principles of God's Word was where she found hope again and was able to conquer all adverse emotions by the Work of God. Today, she is a new creature through Christ Jesus; her mind has been renewed by Almighty Power of God through the baptism of the Holy Spirit in tongues. Now her words are Words of Life, she no longer speaks of negativity, but the positive Word of the Almighty God.

As a Pastor, professional colleague in the Early Care & Early Childhood Program, and as my Sister in Christ, and a longtime friend whom I dearly treasure and love; I endorse this book, which has been written by the inspiration of the Holy Spirit a book that has the demonstration and manifestation of Power of God in Action in today's world. Her burning desire to seek God through the Word, and seeking His Spirit allowed her to write about what pounders strongly in her heart today. Writing the Psychology In Man will help many to find success and become empowered in their walk in Christ and in life; only through Christ Jesus we can become free indeed.

Rev. Ivette Román De Jesús

PREFACE

Throughout the years, though lately more than ever, I have given much thought and have had grave concern for all of humanity. For all of you whose minds

- Wonder
- Worry
- Fear
- Doubt
- Feel rejected
- Feel abandoned
- Think inside the box
- Think outside the box
- Have you feeling misunderstood
- Have you feeling _____ (fill in the blank)

Have no fear my friend, for there is hope! I pray as you read the book you may find through your everyday life a glimpse of how God has brought you to this point in life and wants to give you more, that you may have complete freedom in Him.

In these days, it appears that humanity is seeking what can be found only in God. Somehow, we refuse to surrender to the precious gift of salvation that has been freely given to us, obtained with a very high price that was already paid through our Lord and Savior, Jesus the Christ of Nazareth. It is my sincere prayer that through the guidance and help of the Comforter, the Holy Spirit, each reader of this book (or listener of the audiobook) will be touched in a unique and personal way that brings complete wholeness with our Father in heaven, where there is nothing missing and nothing broken. I also hope you will gain better discernment in spiritual matters at home, at work, and in every area of your life by having a better understanding of *what it means to have the mind of Christ*, and that you will know it is our Father's will that no one should perish.

Shalom,

L. B. Rodriguez

ACKNOWLEDGEMENTS

I would like to thank all my mentors, teachers, preachers, leaders, psychologists, and speakers who went before me and prepared the way for what is yet to come. I would also like to thank all the people who have personally been part of this journey we call life. Whether good or bad, I have learned from you all.

I would like to thank, most of all, my siblings and my four children, who though during different timeframes of my life, gave me a deeper appreciation in understanding and honoring different personalities under one roof, and keeping my sanity through it all. Joseph, my firstborn, you were the town greeter, addressing everyone you passed as a young child. But then you grew up too fast, and though life hit you hard, you grew to be an amazing man of God—honoring God, honoring Claire, whom I love as my own daughter, and honoring your children. I am so proud of the man you have become.

Alexandrea, my little Alie, defender of mankind, though you always seemed to be in your own little la-la land, I felt I was robbed of much time with you. It all went so fast, and now you are on your own in college. I am at peace, though, because I know you have grown in your personal relationship with God, and as long as we put Him first, everything else falls into place.

Michael, you are now officially a high school senior (class of 2020) and have overcome so many challenges. You have kept your cool both at home and in school in better ways than I did when I was your age. I am so proud of the man you are growing up to be.

Daniela, my little princess Nela, as you enter your sophomore year in high school, I can't help but see so much of myself in you, to the point that it's scary. But it's also good because I believe God will do even greater things through you in your life for your generation. You are a free spirit, wanting to do more and be more, and that is good as long as you always remember to keep God in first place in your life. And remember, if your sneakers look too clean, you're not having fun!

I love you guys so much. You all mean the world to me in ways you can never imagine. There is only one love greater than the love I have for you all, and that is the *agape* love of our Father in heaven.

I would also like to thank the greatest psychologist who walked on earth (though He was never given the title of a psychologist), knowing the heart and mind of man better than anyone, my Lord and Savior, Jesus the Christ of Nazareth. Because He did not come to condemn the world but to save it (John 3:17), and we are to overcome the enemy by the blood of the Lamb and by the word of our testimony (Revelation 12:11). One day, one of my sisters told me she was concerned about me and my walk with God. In my confusion I asked her why, because I was in fellowship with God and could not find myself doing anything without Him. He has been with me and helped me through the best and worst times of my life. Then she said, "Then you are wrong, you are wrong in holding it in because the world needs to know your testimony so they may be encouraged in their own walk with God." Well, Sis, this is my personal testimony in knowing the mind of Christ through my journey in life.

INTRODUCTION

Psychology

The word *psychology*, as defined by *Merriam-Webster's Collegiate Dictionary* on Google, (2019) reads:
1. The science of mind and behavior
2. The mental or behavior characteristics of an individual or group
3. The study of mind and behavior in relation to a field of knowledge or activity

It further explains the root of the word *psychology*, which I felt I knew before I actually knew it (if that makes any sense). Knowing this truth was of great significance to what it means to have the mind of Christ.

The Roots of Psychology

Also as defined by Merriam-Webster's Collegiate Dictionary on Google (Ibid), reads:

The word *psychology* was formed by combining the Greek word *psyche* (meaning "breath, principle of life, life, and soul") with *-logia* (which comes from the Greek *logos*, meaning "speech, word, and reason"). An early use appears in Nicholas Culpeper's mid-seventeenth-century translation of Simeon Partliz's *A New Method of Physick*, in which it is said that "Psychology is the knowledge of the Soul."

Today, psychology is concerned with the science or study of the mind and behavior. Many branches of psychology are differentiated by the specific field to which they belong, such as animal psychology, child psychology, and sports psychology.

chology are differentiated by the specific field to which they belong, such as animal psychology, child psychology, and sports psychology.

1

GROWING UP
WITH
RELIGION

GROWING UP WITH RELIGION

Do not conform to the pattern of this world, but be transformed by the renewing of your mind. Then you will be able to test and approve what God's will is—His good, pleasing, and perfect will.

Romans 12:2

It is amazing what God can do through one person; for example, what God has done and continues to do in and through me. Life was not meant to be as complicated as society and religion have made it. Jesus did not come to bring religion; He came to proclaim the good news, set us free from bondage, heal our hearts and show us a better way of life. He came to show us a way by which, despite our challenges in life, we can find freedom in Him and be made better than what we were before. He knew our mind was our greatest weapon against the enemy and gave His life so that we may know this truth.

As a young child, I remember going to church, and even though I honestly do not remember paying attention to everything being said, I do remember being bothered with the thought of going through the same routine week after week and year after year. It was stand up, sit down, kneel down, sit up, stand up, and so forth. Though the service lasted only an hour, to a young nine-year-old like me, it seemed an eternity. It was apparently the same for many adults there also. I felt something was missing.

As I grew older, I realized the messages on certain days were nearly always the same. I figured it was just in case you missed it the year before. I am sure this was a comfort to many, and even to me up to a certain point. Church was a place to find comfort, familiarity, safety, and strength that could not be found anywhere else. Plus, there were no surprises because you already knew when to sit, stand, and kneel, along with the rest of the routine. Nonetheless, this structure created something deep within my being for more of something; I just did not know what.

Around the age of thirteen, I realized there was more I needed to know, but *what, where,* and *how* I could learn what this yearning was deep within me, I did not know. I became more aware of my surroundings, taking notice of people and different personalities. I would often observe people, along with their behaviors, and was always curious as to the thought processes that had led them to their current reality and situation. When in church, I felt there was much more not being said that could be of some help, but I did not know what it was.

You see, in my church at that time, we were not taught or encouraged to read the Bible. We had a huge Bible at home, but I was told I should not skim through it, even if I did read it. It was a sacred book that had to be taken seriously and read in order. We all depended on whatever the church leader (pastor/priest) said. I'm sure to many it was a convenience not to do the extra work of learning, as opposed to studying and holding on to the living Word, knowing that "then you shall know the truth and the truth shall set you free," as Jesus Himself said in John 8:32.

Because there were so many rules I might misunderstand, I was afraid to even hold the Bible sometimes. But I was a rebellious teen, and I would peek at it anyway because I wanted to know more. I wanted to know this God that many were afraid of. I wanted to know Jesus. I knew there was more to being a Christian, more to learn, more that I could do, and I wanted to know it. However, I was particularly careful with the way I thought about God, because so much fear had been put into me concerning my thoughts. For example, I was afraid to think too much about all my high school crushes for fear I might be zapped away to hell.

I am thankful that overall, I did have a decent experience in church and was given a foundation concerning faith, believing for something and having hope. Sadly, I do not see much of that today, especially in our youth, which is all the more reason I felt led to write this book. If I can help someone, no matter their age, grasp the truth without letting religion, politics, or the educational system get in the way of understanding their own divine truth in Christ, it will all be worthwhile.

In this I am grateful for what I learned, which was at that time a basic understanding of who Jesus was and why He came, so simple and yet missed by many. I believe He came to earth to teach us a new way of thinking. He wants us to be aware of the discouraging voices of people in our spheres of influence, as well as the voices in our own heads, voices that we need to tame and control. We have created so much unnecessary destruction to ourselves and others from thoughts that were not held captive. Thus, they freely created inward damage and eventually outward damage, not only to us but to our children and their children. He wants us to be alert and know that we have an adversary, the devil, who is desperate because he and the other fallen angels are running out of time. There are two kingdoms, the kingdom of Almighty God and the kingdom of satan. Both are in the spiritual realm. Jesus wants us to know we can transform our lives in a better way, creating lives of true freedom in Him. He wants us to live our lives to the fullest here on earth, and not just wait until we get to heaven. Our lives here do not have to be a living hell. Jesus wants us to enjoy the full package of freedom on earth as well as in heaven, but it only happens when we seek to have the mind of Christ and be set free from the schemes of the enemy. This may also be why Jesus said in Matthew 18:18, "...whatever you bind on earth will be bound in heaven, and whatever you loose on earth will be loose in heaven." And so, my journey in life begins to what I thought at the time I had no control over.

While in high school, my friends called me Dear Abby[1] as I became known as "the voice of reason" or the therapist who would not judge. Instead, I would listen and come to a wise conclusion that surprisingly helped many arrive at their own needed answers. I was in awe of the thought patterns we developed as individuals that had been conditioned by our families, religion, culture, and high school itself.

This grew into a passion for me, but I was discouraged by many from following the path to be a counselor, let alone a psychologist. I was told many times not to go learning about thoughts and things of the mind because it was not scriptural, and I was warned that this would open my mind to other, undesirable things. Unfortunately, that did happen, but I came back to the truth in Christ. (I will talk about that in future chapters.) I therefore dismissed the thought of pursuing that career path, but I felt in my heart what others were telling me could not be right. I knew God was all-powerful and all-knowing in everything, including our minds, which were created by Him and belonged to Him because we are His.

Many years later, when I embarked on a path out of religion and into fellowship with God, I kept hearing so clearly, "Be transformed by the renewing of your mind." At this point in my life, I had read so many books that I did not know if that was a biblical quote or a quote from one of my favorite authors or motivational speakers. All I knew was that I kept hearing it over and over as I tried to take an afternoon nap. Like any curious person would do, I Googled it. And what do you know? There it was all along, Romans 12:2: "Do not conform to the pattern of this world but be transformed by the renewing of your mind. Then you will be able to test and approve what God's will is—His good, pleasing and perfect will."

What a relief to my soul that was. For many years, I had felt like I didn't belong because I thought differently, even from my own family (I was used to that part). But all along, deep in my heart, I knew there was more to the coming of Jesus than what had been taught to me in the church. I had always believed this, to the point that one day as I sat on my bed, I called out to Jesus as if I really knew in my being that He would be there. I remember feeling confident He would be there, but humbly requested His presence by saying, "Jesus, have a seat; we need to talk." I then poured out my concerns to Him on what I had been taught in church and what I had seen in religious, defeated Christians. I said, "Please do not see it as me being disrespectful." I had respect for church leaders and missionaries, but I just could not fathom the thought of Him accepting such a cruel, torturous, and humiliating death so I could live an okay life.

The sad truth is that religion, with its rules that are not even found in Scripture, has led so many people farther from God rather than closer. There needs to be something within ourselves that knows there is a God out there who really loves us beyond what we can ever imagine. I knew there had to be more, and I wanted to know more. I did not want the okay life. I wanted to know God in heaven and Jesus the Son in a deeper way. I was not yet aware of the power or person of the Holy Spirit.

After making that statement to Jesus, I waited in silence for a bit and felt an overwhelming peace, and I felt deep in my being that I was to "get ready for the journey to know Me." And I must say, what a journey it has been.

However, nothing happened until I accepted a different mind-set, knowing that I was never meant to fit in because God was doing something in my life. I needed a lot of alone time with Him—time to grow closer and dependent on Him. In doing so, my mind was gradually renewed, and I became someone different, though still with many imperfections. As time passed, I learned He was not looking for perfection; He was looking for someone who was willing—willing to be His hands and feet on the earth; willing to grow and overcome obstacles no matter what society and circumstances threw at them; willing to get their hands dirty to help someone in need; willing to do one of the hardest things to do today, that is, greet someone with a warm smile or call someone who may need to hear words of comfort. He looks for those who are not using their conditions and situations as excuses but are willing to take on a new way of thinking and doing that in return brings a new way of living a fulfilling life.

I grew hungry for more so I could help others, especially our youth, but I knew if I wanted to help them, I needed to start with their parents. I remembered years ago asking both a psychologist and a youth pastor/counselor on separate occasions about the challenges they faced with youth today. Ironically, both said parents wanted their children fixed but were not willing to change their own ways. Today, almost twenty years later, that still seems to be the case. There are so many of our youth crying out for help and feel so lost. School bathrooms are now filled with inspirational messages, I believe it's because of the many youth who go to cry and need a message of hope.

However, it is not until a parent is willing to change their own ways by allowing a new mind-set that they are able to help their children, and at the same time help themselves. They need to be free from old hurts and trauma, as well as the spirit of rejection that is the root cause of so many different problems today. It is hard to dig in to past hurts, but if we want to fix today's behavior that is pushing people away from us, we need to dig into the root of it all so that it will not spread to our children and others we really want to love, and not hurt as we have been hurt.

You see, we cannot expect new and better things in life until we ourselves are willing to change from within to receive what we want. We also must be willing to let go of a lot of our past ways of thinking and old ways of doing things so that we may be able to embrace the new life in Christ. This new life with His truth may feel unnatural at first because it is new to us, but like with everything else, we need to practice accepting it. This new life in Christ is a life that can save us, as well as our families and many around us who will eventually want what we now have in Jesus. We need to be armed and dangerous with The Word of God for our kids, our family and ourselves. It can be a scary step to take, but it is a much-needed step worth taking, as we set ourselves and others free when we do so. Much of the problems I have noticed through the years have been weak Christians that did not take authority over the enemy and therefore allowed for generations of defeat. All that can change for future generations in our home, family and neighborhoods as we take the authority that has been given to us through scriptures.

We need to also share our story to help others who may benefit from our testimony. Our story can be the key to their prison that sets them free from bondages that possibly came from many generations past, though they did not know it. However, they now have the power to help future generations.

Think back in your own life. What are some beliefs and thoughts you still hold on to even though you now follow a different path? Are there certain areas of defeat in your bloodline? Are you willing to let go of the ones that you know keep you in bondage, and be set free?

NOTES

2

REPENTANCE
AND
HIS WORD

REPENTANCE AND HIS WORD

The Lord is not slow in keeping His promise, as some understand slowness. Instead, He is patient with you, not wanting anyone to perish, but everyone to come to repentance.

2 Peter 3:9

For many years, every time I heard or even thought of the word *repent,* I pictured someone running madly through a crowd, telling people to repent. It was like in the cartoons when a guy is saying, "The end is coming—you must repent!" Yet the word *repent* may not necessarily relate in the same way as we may be used to hearing.

In the Bible, the word *repent* is always used in relation to sin. It was not until I asked the Lord for a better understanding of the living Word that this was revealed to me, not just once but several times within a week, from different sources. Some may say that was just a coincidence, and it is all right for them to think that. I believe, however, that God is more than willing to reveal to us what we ask so that we may have better a understanding, but we also must be willing to quiet our minds to listen for His voice.

Yes, I did say listen for His voice! The God of the Bible is still the same God of yesterday, today, and forever. He still speaks and wants to fellowship with us. Whether you want to believe this or not, He wants to know about your day, what your troubles are and what you are thankful for. You may say, "He is God and He knows it all." You are right; He is God and He does know it all. However, my friend, when you talk to God from the heart and bring your concerns to Him and thank Him for being with you in this journey called life, you are acknowledging His presence in your life. You are also acknowledging your awareness of what's going on in your life and what exactly you want. That, my friend, can be a life-changer, because with this awareness, you begin to recognize there are things you could never accomplish on your own.

When we look at the word *repent*, we're actually referring to the Greek word *metanoia*, which means a radical change of mind. Not until we have that radical change of mind are we able to better understand who we are, what we can do, and what God truly wants for us. We can quote Jeremiah 29:11 all we want, but not until we absorb deep into our being and experience that radical change in mind-set will we be free. It is then that we can live and understand "...he that the Son sets free is free indeed" (John 8:36).

We were not meant to live lives of hopelessness and bondage. Jesus came, not for us to find religion, but for us to have fellowship with our Father in heaven, a Father who loves us with an *agape* (unconditional) love. He wants nothing but the best for us. Our minds cannot begin to fathom a love so great. Sometimes we look at our lives and wonder if that is true, but trust me, it is, because He is a true expression of love. This is not love as the world sees it, but a true unconditional love, a love that embraces with a warm, comforting, and protective covering that cannot be well expressed, but is felt.

Once you realize this truth, you cannot look back. You will understand what a powerful being you were created to be. Look back in history at the many people who had little to no official education and were criticized and mocked by friends and family, yet created great inventions used to this day. Though some but not all became wealthy, they were all recognized for their accomplishments achieved with little to no education, and sometimes despite an abusive upbringing. They were still great masterminds.

When we read 2 Peter 3:9, we likely can recall many times when we thought God was slow to action. We wanted our prayers answered instantly, yet He did not hurry to answer our prayers and petitions. Maybe this was not because He did not want to answer them, but because we needed to believe that we could receive what we were asking for. Not until we had a radical change of mind and attitude toward the situation did circumstances start to shift in our lives.

I remember when my second child, Alexandrea was graduating middle school I could not find my ticket to enter the school for the ceremony. I was feeling so low in that moment, honestly wishing I were dead. Her father came to take her to school while I got ready. I remember being in the shower hearing voices saying what a bad mother I was and how she will never forget or forgive me. Then that radical moment hit me and I said, "Wait! Am I not a child of the Most High God? Devil, you are a liar, I am going to that school and I will see my daughter graduate up close." And guess what happened? I went to the school and it was as if they were waiting for me and made way so I could be up close to the stage. I was standing but at an angle where I could see all the children very well, including my baby girl. You see, I'm not so tall and even sitting down sometimes I can't see over some people, but that radical change in me that moment of feeling despair and defeat allowed me to see my child graduate. Praise God!

God knows the hearts and minds of man, and in this He is looking at our *why*. What are the reasons why you ask for certain things? James 4:3 says, you do not have because you ask with the wrong motives. So ask yourself, my friend, is it for the good of all concerned, or is it for your good only? Will this particular thing really make you happy, or will it eventually destroy you or those near to you? You see, it is not that God does not want us to enjoy life; He really does want us to enjoy and live life to the fullest. But He did give us free will, and it is up to us whether we let go of self and accept what He has for us. Several times in the scriptures we read of all that He has for us, not just in heaven but here on earth also.

There are countless stories of people's lives being forever changed because of a radical change of mind with an unwavering faith in what they wanted. Some grew tired of being sick and tired, making a sudden shift in thought to choose to be well. Others tired of not having money and made a radical change of mind to do something that would forever change their circumstances and their lives. They never looked back to their old ways of thinking because they now had a new mind-set that made no room for the old.

Of course, for this to come to fruition, there must be a mind shift with determination to complement what the person desires, and it has to come with a resolve from deep within to never go back to the old ways. If the mind-set is not fully established, it will be like some people who hit the jackpot, only to lose it all shortly afterward. Though they suddenly achieved wealth, they still held on to a mismanagement mind-set. On the other extreme are people who make a great amount of money, lose it, and gain it all back, constantly on a roller-coaster of an inconsistent ride with their finances. It all goes back to the mind-set.

In allowing yourself to grow with the mind-set of having "the mind of Christ," you will learn that all you have wanted has been there all along within you. You just have to activate it by making yourself open to receive what you ask for, staying well focused in your mind on what you are really desiring in your heart. We can verbally or mentally ask for one thing and then think or say to ourselves there is no way that can happen, at least not for us. This is true not only for finances, but also for other areas of life. In doing this, we are sending mixed signals and not allowing ourselves to be well positioned for what we want to receive. This is what James 1:8 means when referring to the double-minded person who is unstable in their ways and tossed back and forth in the sea by the wind.

In all this, we must be diligent to our ways so that we do not unintentionally invite other practices that do not glorify our God. I tell you this because I myself went through a phase where I thought it was all about my positive thinking and my doing, not realizing I was trusting God for some things but trying to take care of other things on my own. I was failing to completely consider that He is the omnipotent, omniscient, omnipresent, and an all-loving God.

Then there is that false teaching of certain things we need to wear and keep around and on us for extra protection, as if God needs help because He is not enough. We need not seek other things to help Him; in fact, many of these things can be deceiving, opening doors to a path

away from God as opposed to closer to God and our purpose. It is also crucial to know the God we worship, and
honor is the God of the Bible and not a god we create to
benefit our own individual needs. Take a short break and
look at yourself, your office, your kids and home. Is there
anything on or around that may be representing a false
protection from God?

Friend, ask yourself, what is it that you want? What
are the desires of your heart? Be clear on what you want.
You may say, "God knows my heart and what I want."
And yes, He knows your desires and your heart, but He is
waiting on your acknowledgment of them. This can only
happen in heartfelt fellowship with Him, coming to the
Father as a child. Your thoughts and ideas may seem far
out of reach, but they were put in you for a reason. You
can accomplish them, because you can have the mind of
Christ with a better understanding of the wisdom of the
Holy Spirit.

Some will make fun of you and criticize you, and that
is okay because they are not going where your dream is
taking you. Keep in mind, as 1 Corinthians 1:27 says,
"God chose the foolish things of the world to shame the
wise." If you learn to shut those voices out, you will one
day have the last laugh if you do not give up but just keep
moving forward. Some may criticize your thought pro-
cess because you are not thinking the way they think you
should be thinking, and that, too, is all right. They are not
meant to understand because the vision and thought pro-
cess were God's gift to you, not them. They have their
own gift, but unfortunately, they may miss it because
they are too busy criticizing yours. Do not waste time trying to prove yourself to them; that can be draining. Instead, do as it says in the Scriptures: "Let us not become

weary in doing good, for at the proper time we will reap a harvest if we do not give up" (Galatians 6:9).

Keep in mind also that if you do not act on your dream and calling, someone else may get the call or dream and be the one to act on it. Life can and will go on, and if you choose by your free will to let your dream go, it will go to someone else. My friend, life is too short to hang on to those bothersome thoughts of "could have," "should have," and "would have." Don't let someone else take the opportunity that has been put in your heart. The grave is full of many people who never acted on their dreams, talents, and ideas. My friend, do not let that be you. Take a short break and look at yourself, your office, your kids and home. Is there anything that may be representing a false protection from God?

NOTES

3

WHERE DID THAT
COME FROM?

WHERE DID THAT COME FROM?

When the student is ready, the teacher will appear.
                                    --Author unknown

Many years ago, when I was new in the medical field and growing in my spiritual journey, I was telling a friend of mine how we can read a book, even the Bible, and something new can be revealed to us at that particular time in our lives. At this time, I heard for the first time the phrase *when the student is ready, the teacher will appear*. It's a quote that is so true. Once you take the initiative for radical change in your life, some people will leave. That is all right, because you need to recognize their season has ended and a way is being made for new teachers to come into your life.

The reason I say "teachers" is that there is always something to learn from those who step into our lives, even if only for a brief time. Some will teach us patience, because they will test ours. Some will teach us about pride, because they will make us question our own. Some may teach us to love, like a spouse or our children, when we choose to love them after they are no longer lovable. Some may even teach compassion, because they will touch our hearts in ways that can't be explained. Everything and everyone comes with a purpose.

A sudden new interest sparking in our lives may lead us into a greater future. Suddenly we see a book, a billboard, or even some random commercial confirming this new path for us. It is imperative that we remain alert to what we are giving our attention to, and not make room for distractions. Even more importantly, we must make sure it is from God. There are many ways we can be deceived if we do not have our guard up and are not well planted in the Word of God. I myself have fallen into that trap, not realizing that in wanting to know more of God, I let myself be entertained by other things and ideas that are very common in the world today but not of Him.

My sudden spark of unexpected interest came when I picked up my youngest two children from the daycare center across the street from the hospital where I worked. It was December 1, and we received a notice saying the center was going to close on December 31. You can imagine the horror for us as parents during the holiday season, having to look for a new daycare facility. Parents were in tears and desperate, yet somehow, I felt tranquility deep in my being. I felt something more was to come, and sure enough, I was right.

After I went to sleep that night, I woke up at 5:30 a.m. and looked up at the sky and said, "Lord, I'm going to open a daycare?" I was in a bit of a shock, but I also knew I loved and cared not just for children, but also for the many young parents who were not bad parents but just needed some help and direction with raising their children. I knew I had something to bring to the childcare business; after all, I was also a mentoring mom. I had a clear vision of the many things I could do differently from what I was currently seeing done, from staff development to childcare itself. I then said in my conversation with God, "If You think I can do this, let's do it!"

It was like a different movement taking place, I started meeting new people who allowed for this project to take place. There were mistakes along the way, and many tears, but I accepted them as teaching moments. They did make me grow stronger and wiser in many ways. Every time I was tempted to give up, I would look back and know I could not give up because I already had come so far.

Many tears were shed, and my finances were suffering as I tried to put this project together. Unfortunately, the town where the business was located did not have the most honest people, yet as I stayed connected to God, He sent the right people to help me. The Lord gave me the strength to keep going, and I did. Despite the many dishonest town regulators, God put amazing people in my path to guide me in what was truly needed for safety, and not just "because." I was insistent that the daycare be located in this town, because this was where I had grown up, and I knew the specific needs of my community. I wanted to help and serve. I also knew the daycare needed to be a private facility because I wanted to pray with those parents who desired that. I knew if it was part of the school system that would pose a problem.

During all this time, I was still working in the hospital. One of the doctors asked me what had made me want to open a daycare. When I told him of my early morning wake-up call with God, he said that the difference between me and about a million of other people was that I acted on my desire. Many people get ideas, but they just pass them off as ideas and never act on them. Then they wonder what would have happened if they had at least tried. The doctor's words were truly an inspiration I needed at that moment to keep pushing, and I was able to open my daycare, which later became my ministry of almost 10 years.

I say "ministry" because it truly became a ministry, and it all started with breaking me. One night I was home reading the Bible when I broke down in sobbing tears like a baby, asking God, *why*? Why did I have to go through such hard times, broken relationships, and difficulties in raising my children? Then, as clearly as can be, the Lord said, "What you are going through is because no priest can say, 'I know what you're going through.'" This made sense, since the area where the daycare was located was a predominantly Catholic neighborhood, and there was more God wanted to bring outside of the church walls in that area.

Sure enough, a month after opening the daycare, I found myself sitting with a parent who was in tears as she shared with me her challenging situation. When I heard myself say to her, "I know how you feel," I remembered the night of my breakdown with God. Things may not make sense at the moment you are going through them, but if you look back at your life, I'm sure you will see pieces to the puzzle that make up what your life is today.

It all started to make sense to me, because years earlier, I was unable to take part in classes for mentoring the youth in our church. I was reminded of the exact words said to me, "You are divorced, and therefore what kind of an example would you be, because you cannot take communion with them?" But oohhhh! What a mighty God we serve! He had a much greater plan for my very limited mind, as that was the beginning of my daycare ministry. I had wanted to let youth know how great our God is by teaching them prayers and scriptures so they could go to their next level in faith. However, that would have limited what God wanted me to do, as well as the number of people I would impact.

You see, I would have been teaching only a few of the youth in my church that they needed to follow a religious ritual to be better religious people. However, through the daycare, I had access to several hundred of our young people. These confused and hurt youth were not only high school students, but also parents. Some of the parents who stand out include one young girl who came to me with two children, and she was only a senior in high school. I know that was not easy. She said I was the only one who cheered her on to continue school and not give up or condemn her for her past mistakes. She even invited me to her high school graduation. Knowing how we can impact others in simple ways is priceless.

Another parent was a young girl who, any time she fought with the baby's father, did not want him to see the child. In a loving way, I brought to her attention the fact that for his age this young man was a very responsible father, making sure she and the baby lacked nothing. I felt I needed to bring more counseling to the situation, because I did not want them to fall into the statistics of this world. We talked more of the details and the challenges in relationships and parenting. One month later they were married, and years later we were still in touch and they were still together.

In case you did not notice, many of my parents were the youth of the community. God had a greater plan for me outside the church. I was not perfect, but I was willing to serve outside the church walls and away from the religious group that did not find me fit to minister to their youth. In response, God used me to minister to hurting and disoriented youth, and we had plenty of them.

So many things started falling into place with the parents, children, and staff. For example, I needed staff with the teaching credentials that I lacked. Sure enough, when I prayed for it, the Lord sent me a teacher who was also a pastor and mentor to me, and interestingly enough, years later she performed the wedding ceremony for my first son and his wife. I also had to take a course to be the director of the facility, and the instructor who taught the course also continued to be a mentor to me for many years after the course was over. Today, over 10 years later, 2019 she is a good friend, and has helped and encouraged me with the making of this book.

And it all started with a glimpse, a thought, an idea, or whatever you want to call it that woke me up that one night. I focused on its creation, and I was specific concerning the end result. Not knowing how it was going to happen, but believing that it would, I remembered what Jesus said in Mark 11:24, "Whatever you ask in prayer, believe that you have received it, and it will be yours."

Can you think of a time when you made a conscious attempt to attain something specific and you started seeing or hearing things that related to it, and all the right doors started opening for you? We must make sure that what we seek is in alignment with God's will for us, especially in how we attain it. We must make sure God, through Christ Jesus and His Holy Spirit, is our only source, keeping in mind that He does not need help from any other sources or spirits. He will send the right people at the right time to help us in what we need.

NOTES

4

DON'T LET LIFE JUST HAPPEN TO YOU

DON'T LET LIFE JUST HAPPEN TO YOU

This day I call heaven and earth as witnesses against you that I have set before you life and death, blessings and curses. Now choose life, so that you and your children may live.

Deuteronomy 30:19

M any times, when I think about free will, I think about the character who has an angel on one shoulder and the devil on the other shoulder, both trying to convince the character to choose their suggestion for how to respond to a certain situation. Notice I said "suggestion," because we were given the free will to choose. Sometimes the choices are obvious, but many times they are not. There may be times when we act on our own impulses, and other times when we respond to our gut feelings. There are also times when we take the advice given to us; and other times when decisions are made for us, but we are not aware of that because we are not as active in our thought life as we should be. We fail to realize that some people have us in mind to manipulate us for their own purposes, sometimes for good and sometimes for not so good.

I remember in Catherine Ponder's book, *Dynamic Laws of Prosperity*[2], she realized she was not as active in her own creative life as she should be. When she looked at her car that matched her husband's car, she realized it was his ideal car, but nothing she really cared for. It hit her then that she was not actively creating what she wanted for herself, and therefore someone was creating her life for her with their thoughts. We must learn to be active in our own lives and be able to create for ourselves what we want. Of course, if we do not know what we want, someone else may create it for us, but it will not always be for our good as they may speak negative words over us as well as our loved ones that can harm future generations. We have to keep in mind that we have been given the free will to think and make decisions. We also have a Helper whom Jesus promised would guide and comfort us, and that is the person of the Holy Spirit.

Through the hard way, I have learned two important truths in making decisions. First, never decide under pressure to do something that can wait, even if the person on the other end is not willing to wait; and second, never make a decision when you are tired or hungry. It is like the Snickers commercial, "You're not you when you're hungry." It is imperative to be in the right state of mind when making decisions.

I cannot emphasize enough the importance of prayer, waiting on God, and the guidance of the Holy Spirit. In the end, that gut feeling or intuition, as opposed to a quick impulse, can make a world of a difference. Yes, I know as a first responder of many years, there are life-threatening situations that need immediate action, but overall, too many people make quick decisions that are costly or alter their lives forever. No matter the circumstance, we should ask God to help us make the right decision as well as provide His guidance both in immediate situations and non-immediate ones. For example, in performing my work duties, I often prayed to get the needle in on the first attempt so I would not hurt my patients, and so on. He has never failed me, and I believe He never will fail me, praise God!

In my own experience, I have been in situations where I was pressured to make a business decision without adequate time to think the situation through. I was put on the spot to respond and sign at once. In those situations, I gave my free will away by allowing someone else to choose those decisions for me, decisions that I know now could have waited. Those choices were costly because I did not have much experience from a business perspective, and they ended up costing me several thousand dollars and hurting those I love along the way with a financial burden. It was bad, but it was an expensive lesson learned. This is especially true when it affects your business, your home and family. Many can get hurt along the way, and they did.

Looking to God for wisdom to make better decisions has led me to listen to the lectures of successful people who have also made mistakes yet overcame their losses. I have also read and made sticky notes of scriptures on wisdom. The book of Proverbs is loaded with many useful nuggets for everyday life, instructing us in using our free will to make better choices. That way, we won't lose what matters most, as King Saul did by being impatient and not waiting for the prophet Samuel to arrive before offering the burnt sacrifice to God, as the Lord had commanded him to do (1 Samuel 13).

It is unfortunate today to see the many consequences from free will being exercised with so much lack of discipline and self-control. In my many years of observation, I have noticed much of today's lack of discipline comes from a sense of entitlement, and unfortunately, a great amount coming from our younger generations. Additionally, young rebellious kids from this and past generations, who do not want to receive direction from their parents or anyone else. Then they have their own kids, and now you have the blind leading the blind. The work ethic has also declined in the past several years, something horrible and quite honestly scary. To see a person walking in to start their shift already in a bad mood does not set a good pace for the environment. People come to work with the thought of doing just enough and cannot grasp the thought of going above and beyond. This is because they only see their work as what their salary equates, as opposed to being an exceptional employee who wants to feel good about the work done. At first, I thought these were just my observations, but when there were many people who also pointed them out, I knew something had to change. Especially in patient care, it is imperative to create a positive environment for our staff that are hands on with patients.

It can be scary, and we may be tempted to choose fear in this age because we are bombarded with so many things in the news and social media that insist on putting fear and insecurity in our paths. But oh, how wonderful our God is that many years ago, He supplied a way for us to choose either life or death, blessings or curses and He even urged us to choose life (I suggest you read Deuteronomy 30). You see, to have the mind of Christ is to know that we have a choice and a loving Father in heaven who wants to bless us. Nonetheless, there are principles and laws we must apply to better align ourselves so that we can receive the many blessings in store for us. Not man-made principles and laws, but scriptures that still hold true today. And yes, my friend, I did say "blessings," because our God is still looking for those He may bless. We must understand that both blessings and curses are vehicles of the supernatural and we serve a supernatural God.

The news and media may try to scare us with their own insecurities and fears, but if we learn to ground ourselves in the living Word, we can go through this journey called life knowing that our Father in heaven has our backs. As He Himself has said, He will never leave us or forsake us (Deuteronomy 31:6; Hebrews 13:5). Again, this all boils down to the free will given to us. Do we seek His guidance and help when we need it, or do we rely on ourselves?

So, what will you do with your free will? Will you use it to make better decisions for yourself and your sphere of influence? Will you use it to create a better life, or will you use it to destroy your life? You now know you have a choice to make with the free will you have been given.

You do not have to try to change the whole world. The good news is, it is not your job to change the entire world, but you can play your part. When you become a better person in Christ, you will radiate it to others so that they might want what you have, and in turn contribute their part to the world. That is just a small part of using your free will to create a piece of your best to share with others. You don't have to start big; it can be something simple, even if it is just a shared, sincere smile. That smile you give someone can be a life changer for many. However, not all will receive it; I remember a woman in the supermarket complaining as she pushed her cart through the isles that someone smiled at her. I was just hoping the person that gave her the smile wouldn't feel discouraged to continue smiling because of the lady's reaction. I had mixed emotions there I must admit. I thought it was funny to see the lady's reaction yet sad because it was something foreign to her.

To have the mind of Christ, I believe, also means being present so that our free will is not easily usurped by others. Stand firm in the Word, my friend, so that you are not easily tossed to and fro, letting years go by where you live in regret because you let others choose for you. It is unfortunate, but many times this happens right at home. For example, when I went back to school, I was complaining about the demands of being a single parent and juggling life. My school counselor listened and then finally said, "Require your children to be respectful of your time." At first, I must admit, I thought she just didn't get it, but the more I thought about it, the more it made sense. I began putting her advice into practice.

I also learned not to be impulsive with a seemingly good spur-of-the moment idea. Many times, after a two-minute thought, I realized it wasn't such a good idea. I also learned to say no. Yes, I live to help others, but even Jesus had to get away from everyone and everything to be alone in the Father's presence. We all need to renew and refresh ourselves from the demands of life. That, my friend, is having control of your own free will.

NOTES

5

WATCH OUT FOR
DREAM-KILLERS

WATCH OUT FOR DREAM-KILLERS

Being confident of this, that he who began a good work in you will carry it on to completion until the day of Christ Jesus.

Philippians 1:6 NIV

Is it safe to tell you to go confidently in the direction of your dreams, or have your dreams been replaced by nightmares, fears, and cares of the world? Or, are you living someone else's dream? Have you taken many detours that somehow brought you back to the direction of your dreams? Christ is in the business of transformation to help us reach our dreams. Unfortunately, there are dream-killers along the way.

These dream-killers do not always come from family; some come from teachers or other people we have looked up to and have profound respect for. Do not get me wrong—there are many amazing teachers out there, and I pray every year for God to continue to give them wisdom and patience, not only with their students, but also with fellow faculty and parents. I also pray for a special blessing in their personal lives, because I know they do not have it easy. I pray they may always remember why they became teachers in the first place. I know salary is not the biggest reason; I believe they are underpaid for all they must deal with, especially in today's world.

I remember the sadness of my son's friend concerning an art project he was originally very proud of, until the art teacher embarrassed him in front of everyone. The teacher remarked that his artwork was ugly and asked what he was thinking, while also giving him a zero on it.

He did not want to mention it to his mother for fear of being further embarrassed. My daughter, when in high school, was incredibly sad because she had to write an essay, and even though she had her own idea of what to write, she knew if she wanted a good grade, she had to write something that would appeal to her teacher.

My own personal experience of a dream-killing teacher was with my high school guidance counselor. I do believe she meant well, but she was very discouraging when it came to my future. She told me I would not make it in the health field (while drafting this book, I have been in the health field for more than twenty years). She said it would be too hard for me and gave me a list of quicker and easier career choices. I insisted, however, that I wanted to give it a shot to make it in the health field. For parents with rebellious teens, this kind of discouragement can actually work for good, because it can bring out a determination to seek their dreams.

As if that was not bad enough, every semester when I was in college and tried to register for my next classes, I was discouraged from pursuing my path and advised to take easier classes so I could make money more quickly. I felt deep inside, however, that was not right. Even though I did not have many role models to speak life into me, I did have a select few (one being my sister), of much wisdom, and that was good enough. I was also rooted in my heavenly Father, and that led me to believe I could do more. Honestly, it was very challenging, because at that time not much attention was given to learning disabilities and learning styles, not to mention the fact that I was in an abusive marriage. But I had one thing going for me, and that was the determination to finish my course and provide a better future for my family.

You see, I was a very slow reader and learner. You would never know with the many books I possess today because I did not give up on myself with wanting to learn more.

When my grades dropped from 4.0 to 2.35, I was called in for a review to see if I was going to be allowed to stay. I had to give an explanation of what was going on in my life to cause my grades to drop so quickly. I explained to them that I knew, despite my challenges at the time, that if I took a break, I might never come back. I knew I had to stick with it through this inconvenient situation because my life truly depended on making a better future for myself, and my son, who was at that time one year old.

You see, I was married, but there was a lot of mental and verbal abuse going on and unlike physical abuse, mental and verbal abuse is not always so obvious. The man even had my family against me because he was such a fun-loving man in front of everyone, but behind closed doors it was a nightmare. Beginning with the day we came back from our honeymoon. The moment we walked in the house, his first words were, "Now you are going to know the real me." I wanted to think he was just joking, but I felt hit with a sudden fear. As time passed, I thought it was just me not handling marriage as a woman should. You know, working full-time, coming home late sometimes after work, cooking and everything else that went with it, because as he said to me, "No one will ever love you like I do." I felt trapped living with this man that I felt was at the time demonic and dangerous. He cursed out saints I never knew existed. After listening to Evangelist John Ramirez's[3] testimony; an ex-satan worshiper who then gave his life to Jesus, it all made a lot of sense to me. You see, one day when my first son was maybe three months old and barely moving in his crib, I heard a little noise in the room and felt I had to go check on him. To my horror I saw my baby in the crib with his little hospital blanket twisted around his neck as if it were a rope. He did not appear to be hurt and I started praying and crying out to God lifting my son up to Him. I was in deeper trouble than I had realized at the time, yet I also knew God was with me somehow.

This all changed several months later at a time when I had lost several thousands of dollars on doctors who would not listen to me as I kept explaining my discomforts. I remember I would walk the streets and not notice my face was drenched in tears until people were close to me, then somehow, I would awake and touch my face. The doctors kept telling me there was no way I could be pregnant if I had my menstrual cycle punctually every month. Instead, they insisted it was just my imagination because I wanted to be pregnant. This went on until my issue of blood and pain became so horrible it landed me in the hospital, and guess what? I was six months pregnant, weighing 103 pounds, down from my normal 120.

I was sent home and told to have complete bed rest. Instead, when my sister brought me home, I went to the room and threw myself on the floor and cried and cried and continued crying like a sobbing baby. I cried out to God and told Him I did not want to have another child from that man, especially since this pregnancy was from an unwilling act. I remember crying out and saying, "I just want another chance at life to live and to be the mother that my son needs me to be for him." I then felt myself wrapped in such an amazing love that words cannot begin to explain. I believe it was the Agape love of

Christ Himself. I say June 24, 1993 was the day I was born again, because I felt new life in me, with great boldness.

Thinking back now, it was like the woman with the issue of blood who touched the hem of Jesus' garment. There was definitely something powerful there, except that mine was for a few months as oppose to years and it was followed the next morning by a pain that was worse than labor itself. My husband at the time knew I was in pain, but left anyway, and my sister came back to take me to the hospital. They immediately put me on the stretcher. I remember and think it's funny now how, even with all the pain I was having, I made sure to personally call my boss and let him know I was not able to come to work that day. Can you imagine his confusion? Several days after the miscarriage, I was let out of the hospital, broke up with my husband, went to work and tried to continue my classes. I did not let those obstacles kill my dreams of living and serving.

Thankfully, I was given another chance. With this opportunity came a deeper walk with God and a greater desire to know Jesus in a deeper and clearer way. You see, there is always a light at the end of the tunnel. Though my life appeared to be crumbling and falling apart, it was actually falling into place, making me a better person than I was before.

When I was doing my internship in the hospital, I had a clinical instructor who was incredibly challenging and hardly ever had a good thing to say to her students. Diane was very good, but very tough. We all feared her. One day I had a patient in end-stage lung disease. She wanted to eat her bran muffin so badly, but it was hard for her to feed herself. She was sad because it was her favorite. I did not know if I as a student should feed her, but my conscience would not give me peace about leaving her. So, when I finished my rounds with two other patients, I came back to her, and I fed and comforted her.

Then my clinical instructor, Diane, called me, and of course, my heart dropped. I thought, "Good Lord, I'm losing my license before I even get it!" But what she said shined light into my darkness. She told me that she had seen what I did, saying that I had what it took to be in health care because I cared. She told me that if she had to choose between me and two other "A" students she was observing, she would choose me, because they skimmed through the patients and only looked at the machines they were attached to, not once looking at the patients themselves. She urged me not to give up and encouraged me to keep trying, saying this world needed more people like me who could see their patients, not just their attachments and numbers.

Today I am trying to track this woman down, because I need to personally thank her for speaking life into me. At the time of writing this book, she had moved out of state. I was told she was too tough, and many students thus complained too much. Many of the new generation of students who followed my class were not appreciative of that tough-love teacher. They wanted the grade, but not the lessons in caring for humanity.

This woman spoke life into me and did not even know it. Still to this day, I am thankful for her words. As I let her words sink deep inside my heart, I went to church and knelt before the Lord. giving Him my hands, I said, "Lord, these are Your hands that want to serve You and help Your children. If You feel You can trust me with Your children, please help me pass my exams and give me the mind to better absorb what I am studying, and if You ever feel I need to change the path, I will."

Never underestimate the power of prayer, because as short and simple as that prayer was, it came from deep within my being, a true cry to God. At once things began happening. That prayer moved mountains in my life! One instructor started to take my tests away from me before I could second-guess my answers and get them wrong. Then, out of nowhere, he began giving me case scenarios with patients, and I gave him the answers he needed to hear. Fellow classmates started to come over and study with me. I passed every exam and even passed my board exam on the first shot!

I still look back in amazement at how good and faithful our God is. He put the right people there at the right time to help me reach my goal. Though I am more of an audiovisual learner, after that prayer, I noticed that my reading and comprehension got much better.

Though there was much discouragement in those beginning years, I learned it is not always teachers or people we look up to who are the dream-killers in our lives. Sometimes these dream-killers are right in our own homes with us, trying to bring us down. Pray for them, but keep in mind that the challenges prepare us for the difficulties we will face out in the world.

And then there are times when we are our own dream-killers, allowing voices and thoughts in our minds to keep us from fulfilling our true God-given potential. We can be particularly good at killing our own dreams if we give in to discouraging words from ourselves or others that do not align with the Word of God.

Some may mean well, but we just need to love them anyway without sharing too much of our dreams with them, so they won't ruin it for us.

NOTES

6 { LIVING UNDER A SPELL

LIVING UNDER A SPELL

Be sober-minded; be watchful. Your adversary the devil prowls around like a roaring lion, seeking whom he may devour.

1 Peter 5:8

Many Christians, especially the super-duper religious ones, are very afraid of hypnotism and spells. The very words freak them out. I know because I have witnessed it myself many times. The unfortunate reality that many fail to realize is that they (myself included) have allowed themselves to come under a spell or be hypnotized by what they have allowed themselves to believe, whether as children or as adults. For example, we accept negative words spoken over our lives as children, or even before birth, to come to fruition. Or maybe the trauma of an abuse has caused crippling fear, intimidation, low self-esteem, or other limiting and paralyzing feelings and beliefs. All these are rooted in a spirit of rejection, and years later their truth may still linger in our lives as opposed to the real truth that is given in Scripture. As Jesus said in John 8:32, "Then you shall know the truth and the truth shall set you free."

How about our environment? Whether it is our culture, our family, our work, or our friends, we need to foster greater awareness so that we are not living and accepting the truth of others in our lives as our own. Instead, we need to be living the truth about us that is in Scripture. Look back at your own family tree and ask yourself which traits are common to your family. Is it alcohol, divorce, quarrels, gambling, issues of the heart, diabetes, or other medical conditions? That's not coincidence, because there are spirits and curses (whether recent or generational) trying to keep us in bondage, as well as inherited tendencies in our bloodlines. I know it is a difficult thought for many people to grasp today, even Christians. But think about it. There is no way you can go through the day without hearing or reading something to make you think something is wrong with you that a miracle drug can cure. It will make you feel better or look better or give relief from that particular symptom you may be feeling at the moment, even if it has twenty different side effects, one of which one could be death. Yet somehow the goal is to convince you that this is what you need to have a happy, complete life. Those are all lies being fed to us.

Many situations can put us into a hypnotized state, going through life under a spell even though we do not realize it. I had remarried and divorced again (Tzhat's another story on not waiting on God). One situation that comes to mind was a time when my second ex-husband's son came to visit for two of what were the longest weeks of my life. Everyone who knows me knows I have a special love for children, but this child really tested every bit of my patience He was like Dr. Jekyll and Mr. Hyde. In front of his father, he was very respectful and well behaved, but as soon as the door closed, it was a nightmare. The kid cut my newborn son's clothes. When the baby was sleeping, and he was told to keep it down he would go next to him and yell. Those are just a few of the many things I had to deal with for the most part of those two weeks. I know today my mistake was in keeping quiet, because I wanted my husband at the time to enjoy his son during the time he had him. However, the effect it had on me was traumatic. It was so bad I remember not feeling present in my reality, as if hypnotized or under a spell.

I woke up from this spell one day when we were all out together as a family. I was driving, and even though I was in our neighborhood, I did not know where I was. I was lost. My ex-husband yelled at me, asking me where I was going. I could not answer, but I silently prayed and thankfully I snapped back to reality, and we got home safely. I was maybe two to three miles from our house, but the stress had taken over so badly that I really did not know where I was. That was scary and dangerous. I promised myself I would never allow anyone to drive me to that point ever again. I knew something had to change, but it had to start with me.

An example from a few years ago happened to a dear friend of mine. Though a God-loving Christian, she had never given much thought to keeping her guard up. For no medical reason, she was not able to conceive children and lived in a pattern of brokenness. When realizing there was no medical reason for her not to conceive, and later discovering that an evil-minded ex-girlfriend of her brother had placed a curse on their family, she and her sisters decided to go into deep prayer and fasting. They prayed and fasted not just for curses to be broken off them, but also for the chains that were keeping them in certain bondages. She said at first it was very uncomfortable because there was resistance in the spirit and crazy things started happening. They did, however, know that certain things had to break in order for their lives to be put back into place better than before. Things had to break and leave their lives to make room for the blessings of new things ahead. As for my friend, she now has a beautiful healthy baby boy, and her family is well. To God be the glory!

With the permission of my daughter, I will share another situation that recently hit close to home. It did not happen overnight. The enemy kept peeking in waiting for the right time to make the attempt of devouring my child and praise God, the enemy failed. At the time, one might have thought she was just being a rebellious teen, but in my spirit, I knew that was not even my daughter in that body. She went from light to darkness and everyone kept saying it was just a phase. Seeing her, it seemed like her glow of youth and life had gone out. There was definitely something else trying to take over. She was having many nights of insomnia, and when she did sleep, she would frequently have sleep paralysis. The music she played as well as what she allowed herself to watch, read and hear, were changing her into someone we did not recognize, and unfortunately not in a good way. She no longer talked to the friends she grew up with, and her new friends did not bring a sense of peace when they entered my home. Thank God not all her friends had those vibes of uneasiness and confusion. It was just a selected few. She had one particular poster in her room that gave me discomfort, even though it was just a guy's upper body with tattoos, and I knew it had to be more to that poster because she had another one of a guy smoking, with piercing and tattoos and it didn't give me that same uncomfortable feeling. She also had fabric hanging on her wall that was black and white with zodiac signs, yin-yang, the sun and moon. It bothered me and made me feel very uneasy from the day she got it. I remember going into her room and praying inside and outside, but felt challenged, and I grew to have what I call a holy anger. I would feel chills of fear trying to get a hold of me. I was slowly losing my daughter and was not going to let her go without a fight. I was more afraid of losing my daughter than facing that which was trying to scare and paralyze me with fear.

I reached out to prayer partners and let them know there was a spiritual battle going on with my daughter. I knew that according to Ephesians 6:12 we do not battle with flesh and blood but against rulers and principalities and spiritual forces of evil. I needed to act quickly and started praying. Shortly after that, my older son called me and told me he felt we needed to do some serious warfare prayers in my daughter's room, and it could not wait. That night we took anointing oil, put it on our hands, anointing each other, and began praying in the Spirit (unknown tongues), because as scripture says sometimes, we do not know what we ought to pray for, but the Spirit does (Romans 8:26).

So we prayed around the house and he went in her room, and would you believe, he went directly to the poster and ripped it out, followed by ripping out the wall fabric decoration (I never mentioned to him that those two things bothered me). My daughter of course was upset and did not want to go back to her room. He also took her cell phone and was in deep, angry prayer over it. She told me a few days later how frustrated she was because her phone was not working properly and kept freezing, until she gave up on it and accepted that it wasn't working as well.

One morning before I was leaving for work, as I passed by her door, I felt a presence that seemed to be mocking, as if it had her. It wasn't the music that was playing, but I felt uncomfortable. I placed my hand on her door and started praying and prayed all the way to work. I kept praying in the Spirit as Ephesians 6:18 says, on all occasions with all kinds of prayers and requests. When I got to the parking lot, I got a text from her telling me how she was always messing up on me (those were not her exact words). She felt she was a bad child. I was led to send her a text telling her that she was growing up, and in finding herself she would mess up and it was okay, because I would be there for her because I loved her. She would always be my Little Princess Nela. When I got home that evening, she told me she wanted to go spend time with her father in Puerto Rico. I told her it was fine if she wanted to go. While washing dishes, again I felt in my spirit she wanted to go because she felt she was a burden. I went back to her and told her to please tell me she wanted to go because she wanted to be with her father, and not because she was a burden to me. In this she broke down crying and sobbing, because it was true that she felt she was a burden in my life. The enemy was feeding her mind lies.

She also went on to tell me the text she got earlier that morning, letting her know I loved her, and she will always be my Little Princess Nela, brought her to an awakening. She said that text saved her life. We both cried, and I let her know that I was there for her and we would get through this journey called life together. By the grace of Almighty God, we did! She's still in her journey to find herself. Her walk with God is an individual walk and I know she will have her own encounter one day with Him and know that He is real, and He loves her more than I can ever. Today she is a whole different person, reflecting on how she was and where she is going in life, with a brighter vision for herself. Praise God!

I have learned that arguing and fighting with her was not going to help the situation because she was in another state of mind and did not understand the issue at hand. Because of my discernment and obedience to act on it, with the help of my prayer partners, we were able to break that spell in the name of the Father, Son and Holy Spirit! There was a lot of fasting and prayers day and night. I even had recorded prayers playing in my house at night to keep the fire of prayers going, and there was a divine restoration in my home.

These are just a few examples, but I am sure we can all relate to days when we cannot remember what happened during the day or how we got to work, because we have become immune, as if hypnotized, to our daily routine. The sad and even scary thing is when we allow this to continue day in and day out, or even worse, year in and year out.

Today I look back at that event and I see it as a blessing in disguise, because what the enemy intended for evil, God used for my good (Genesis 50:20). In this I can't help but to grow closer in my walk with and dependence on God in all my difficult situations. He never let me down. Things did not always go as I planned, but I learned His plans were so much better than mine. I also needed to learn to be present and sober-minded, not just let life happen to me, and that I can ask for what I need.

Can you look back to a time—and be honest with yourself—when you were hypnotized or even numb to your environment or situation? You look back and are tempted to ask yourself what you were thinking, and realize you were not really thinking at all, just going through the motions. Can you see it in other people around you?

If you look around, you will see real live zombies walking by. I know, because I was once there too.

Some situations we bring upon ourselves unknowingly, but what about situations we do not realize are the results of spells? What about spells and curses spoken over someone even before they were born? People may carry things that were passed on to them, and though they recognize a pattern, they think that is just how it's going to be. Sadly, curses and spells are not often mentioned today to give people hope in finding their cure down to the root through Scripture. Instead, we try to find hope in TV shows and movies that can create even more harm because we unknowingly make those things our idols. I myself have been guilty of this. Then one day I was listening to the teachings of Derek Prince[4]. I remember listening to one of his lectures on YouTube, "how to pass from curse to blessing". During the prayer part of the video, I started coughing as if trying to throw up. I really felt something coming out of me and it wasn't food. I felt exhausted yet relieved because I knew that spirit which was weighing me down for years finally left.

There is hope, my friend. Take notice if you see patterns in your neighborhood or even your family. Learn to take spiritual inventory, especially in your home and family bloodline. There is hope when we allow ourselves to be renewed with the mind of Christ, allowing Him, through His Holy Spirit, to guide us through prayers and actions so we can be set free, and so our families, our communities, and our spheres of influence can be set free from whatever keeps them under a spell.

I say "actions," because sometimes we may be led to get rid of certain things or objects that we may have bought unknowingly, or they were given to us with the

purpose of destroying us in one way or another. Sometimes what we do in the natural may not make sense, but we must remember that we serve a supernatural God. As Jesus said in Matthew 19:26, "With man this is impossible, but with God all things are possible." I remember asking the Lord to reveal to me what I needed to remove from my house. Interestingly, these things included books and audio lectures, knickknacks. Many things I owned, had to go.

To be free in Christ is true freedom, and we should seek awareness of what is not for our highest good in this life and in the life to come. Through Scripture and an honest, humble, and hungry heart for God, we can have this, because the Lord reveals Himself in His own way and time to whomever He wishes. With so many things happening in this world today, we need to seek Him while He may still be found and call upon Him while He is near (Isaiah 55:6). Time is running out, and it is becoming clearer as the days go by.

My prayer for all of us is that we may truly wake up from whatever is trying to keep us hypnotized or numb to the things of this world, so we may know His perfect plan for our lives. Scripture tells us it is not His will that anyone perish, but that all should come to repentance (2 Peter 3:9). Though for many it may be difficult to grasp and understand, our God is a good God who loves us so much. Eyes have not seen, ears have not heard, nor has the heart of man imagined, what God has ready for those who love Him (1 Corinthians 2:9). Our God is a good God beyond our own understanding.

NOTES

7

FINDING
YOURSELF
IN HIS PRESENCE

FINDING YOURSELF IN HIS PRESENCE

But the helper, the Holy Spirit, whom the Father will send in my name, he will teach you all things and bring to your remembrance all that I have said to you.

John 14:26

The more time passes, the more I have come to realize what an amazing gift has been given to us, yet it is ignored by many Christians. "What gift?" You may ask. The gift known as the Comforter, Helper, Guide, Teacher, Advocate, and Counselor—the Holy Spirit, the third person of the Holy Trinity, who has been left out of many churches. In some churches, He has been replaced by saints, Jesus' mother, and religious rituals, that are not mentioned anywhere in scriptures as being part of our salvation. I was guilty of this at one time myself, because that was how I was brought up and it was at one time a part of me.

I refer to the Holy Spirit as "He" because in Scripture the Holy Spirit is mentioned as the third person of the Holy Trinity and is referred to as "He." However, while growing up, I barely heard of the Holy Spirit except through songs, the sign of the cross, and in church when they talked about the life, death, and resurrection of Christ. Even then, I did not think that much of Him, as He was not mentioned for who He is. I never gave Him much thought until one day when I was about to have a breakdown because of so many things happening from all directions. My kids were being kids in school getting into trouble, my mother was not well, and my ex-husband and I were not on the best speaking terms. In the middle of all this, one of my employees invited me to a weekend retreat in her church.

My first thought and words to her were that I would think about it, but really, I was listening to the voices telling me every reason I should not go because I was already busy. She left me the form to fill out, and I stopped, thought, and wondered, "D*o I go to this with people I do not know, or do I just go to work as I usually do to get occupied in thought?"* I knew something had to change for the sake of my children, my home, and my sanity. I prayed about it. While reasons for me not to go immediately came to mind, I realized my kids were with their father that weekend, and I still had more than enough time to let my job know I would not be in. But most of all, deep inside my being, I knew I needed something to happen.

I prayed for God to take care of my kids, and especially my mother, since I was her proxy at the time and made her medical decisions. Then came the decisive moment. God knew through my prayers that I needed help, and He sent that young girl to issue this invitation that would bring me into a deeper level of faith and a hunger for the things of God. Through this retreat, I came to know Jesus in a deeper, more relational way, despite what my church had taught me.

As we were being welcomed on the first evening of the retreat, we had our keys labeled and put away so that we would not be disturbed, in the event that cars needed to be moved. Cell phones, too, were put away. Oh, my goodness! I thought my life was being taken away from me (I am sure many can relate). I hesitantly relinquished my phone, and it was the hardest yet best thing I ever did.

After that day, I learned to detach myself from the things of this world.

The whole weekend, through prayer, worship, and words from the pastor, I came to know the love of God and compassion for humanity in a way that words cannot explain. It was a love that I never knew existed; yet deep inside had longed for. It was an *agape* (unconditional) love. I cried, not just tears, but what we call "the ugly cry." I cried and yet experienced a peace and joy that was so uplifting and liberating. I can honestly say, I felt lighter. Like Scripture tells us, it was "a peace that surpasses all understanding" (Philippians 4:7). That weekend was an experience I will never forget and will forever be grateful for.

You see, we may get stuck in the busyness of life, and pause for fixes of this world that help temporarily but do not get to the root of our soul. They cannot fill us with spiritual nourishment, giving us strength to face the world. When we allow ourselves to be filled with His presence, however, our situation may not change, but we change. Those things that once bothered us do not even tickle our nerves anymore.

For those who have children and spouses, get ready, because if you seek guidance from your heavenly Father, you will start noticing help coming your way to enable you to handle your situation better. This is when you need to be alert, as you will get your answers to the request for help through TV, a song, an article, a billboard, or some other avenue. When this starts happening, my friend, you will know you are maturing in Christ. There is no reason for anyone to feel hopeless in this world when we have a Father in heaven that is more than willing to send help to us, if we just believe He will.

To have the mind of Christ is to know we are not meant to do life alone. To think that is foolish. Whether we want to admit it or not, we are all connected. In one way or another, we each bring something to the table. I know it is challenging when we are around difficult people, or as I call them, "spiritual vampires" that suck the life out of us. We must understand, however, that those difficult people in our lives may be what we need to grow more in Christ. As we wholeheartedly seek God, He will help us through the wisdom, guidance, and people He sends. We do have to know that it is up to us to ask, seek, and knock (Matthew 7:7–8), but we need to be clear what we are asking, seeking, and knocking for.

That experience in that little church in Paterson, New Jersey, was an experience I will never forget. The church wasn't big and fancy, but it had The Holy Trinity in it. There were many healing miracles, the breaking of chains, and deliverance were experienced by the many women there. It truly was an amazing experience.

Are you in need of deliverance and a closer relationship with God? Pray about it. Ask Him to guide you into true fellowship with Him, as well as lead you to a Holy Bible-based church that honors the Holy Trinity of God. Our Father in heaven is more than willing to lead you on the path that guides you to Him and His truth.

NOTES

8

WHO IS THIS "GHOST", AND HOW IS HE MY HELPER?

WHO IS THIS "GHOST", AND
HOW IS HE MY HELPER?

The Holy Spirit can cast out the evil spirit of the fear of man. He can make the coward brave.

Charles H. Spurgeon

As time passed, I openly admit that I went from that high feeling of freedom and deliverance to becoming comfortable with it and not staying in frequent prayer and in the Word every day, as I knew I should have. I slipped back into the routines of life, letting my spiritual guard down. What many people do not realize, and today I try to communicate to others, is that it is imperative that we keep our guard up so that we do not give spiritual entrance to the enemy (Ephesians 6:10–19).

As time passed, I noticed the pattern starting again, and the challenges of life hit hard. Life tried to get the best of me through those challenges, and they hit harder this time. This was before I knew the importance of keeping myself on guard in prayer, because although I believed I was delivered, I did let my guard down. I can honestly say, as mentioned in Luke 11:24–25, everything came back worse. You name it—I had it. I was tested relationally, financially, emotionally, and spiritually.

For many of us, our first response in these difficult situations is to look at the outside sources that have contributed to the problem. In my case, the reality is that I played a huge role in letting these situations back into my life. Unknowingly, I had provided an opening to these spirits of defeat. I already had a spirit of rejection that had clung to me since before I was even born, but I did not know it. Matthew 12:43–45 explains how we can unknowingly allow such spirits to take hold of our lives. You see, I cleaned house and was made anew when I had that amazing experience of knowing God at a deeper level, but I let myself get too comfortable, and slipped back into my old ways of stinking thinking. I allowed my behavior to make room for those spirits to return, bringing in more negative things to take place in my life. To make matters worse, this continued for several years before a breakthrough occurred. All this happened mainly because I let my spiritual guard down and gave the enemy an entry point into my life and home.

To be clear, we must really know and understand that giving entry to the enemy is not always through dark magic, as some may think. We give entry to whatever we allow ourselves to see, hear, absorb, or bring into our homes and our lives. For example, do we make room to entertain gossip even as we are coming out of church? Do we entertain ourselves with music that clearly makes us feel unworthy or encourages us to hate? Do we allow objects in our homes that may look like nice antiques, yet carry curses with them? We need to be diligent in our ways for our sake and the sake of our homes and family, especially the younger generation that finds itself lost and seeking for truth. We as adults are stewards of the children we have been entrusted with.

In all this, I am extremely thankful for the power of prayer. In many cases, not many of the prayers were mine for myself, but from people I know who kept me in prayer. I can honestly say I would not be alive today if it were not for the prayers of others. Do not get me wrong;

I prayed, but at that time I was not often getting up at two or three in the morning. I was, however, sometimes waking up to pray without knowing for whom or what, just knowing it had to be done, and so I did it.

I knew God had an amazing plan for me, because even though I was making many mistakes, He knew my heart and my *why* in everything. He knew I had a heart for His children and a heart to serve. He also knew that to preserve me, He had to take me away from many people that were pulling me away from Him with busyness of life, and He did. To understand all this, you must see the type of life I was living. I was trying to help others who I knew were worse off than me, but I had a dream to inspire the world. That had to wait, however, everyone else needed me because their situations needing attention, and this included my mother who was not doing well physically at the time and my four children that really did need me. Life was demanding and draining from all angles.

Before my mother went to be with the Lord, she told me she wanted me to move away after she passed. She knew, through her spiritual eyes, more than she wanted to admit, and I learned this afterward. She had the gift of seeing beyond what the natural eye can see but wanted nothing to do with it because she was afraid of it. She wanted to live for God and only God, and she rejected those abilities that could open doors to other things.

Two weeks after she passed, I was called by one of my nieces to see a house that was for rent and see if I would make the brave move and move across the state. I prayed about it and I moved, but the problem was that I brought my old ways with me and it almost killed me. The stress really put me in a bad position where I had to let go of my business. This was my only income at that time since I had put my medical practice on hold. Two weeks later, my teenage daughter got into a car accident. I thank God to this day she only suffered a bruised knee, but my car was not drivable for about a month. The mechanic said it was a miracle my daughter came of that car walking. Because she was so petite, she should not have made it alive were his words. I told him that when you surround your kids in prayer, no weapon formed against them shall prosper (Isaiah 54:17). The weapon had formed, but by the time it came to her, she only got a bruised knee. To God be the glory! The mechanic smiled, shook his head, and said, "I believe it. That definitely was something." The interesting thing was that it happened the day before I was to get water baptism in my church. I left a message for one of the ladies I served with in church, to let her know I did not have a car for that Sunday and would not be able to serve. She called me back, knowing that I was also to get baptized, and said she would come get me and my children. She lived very close to the church and drove forty minutes one way to get us, bring us to Life Church in Lehigh Valley, Pennsylvania and bring us back to New Jersey. Anna and my church family were of great help in getting me back on my feet during those challenging times.

Besides the water baptism and church, everything else was a downward spiral. I ended up giving my things away because I had to leave my home. You may be thinking, *why give it away if you could sell it?* At that time, I felt God wanted me to do the harder thing, which was to give it away. As I was giving away the bigger furniture, a dear elderly friend came to the house and offered her empty house for us to live in and helped me get back on my feet. Today, my son lives there still with his wife and kids. She had been trying to sell it "as is," but she said two weeks prior to offering it to me, she had felt the need to put up new wall panels and carpeting, oil for heat, and a new stove. To God be the glory!

It was a much smaller house, which was perfect because I had already given away the big things from my house. I felt as if I were hidden from everyone and everything, yet I was close enough to the important things I would need, like to do grocery shopping, run errands, and take my kids to school. It still puts a huge smile on my face when I think of that story; God is faithful in His Word, and He promised to never leave us or forsake us (Hebrews 13:5).

After I moved, I slept for three days. I got up to get the kids to school, ate, went to the bathroom, and slept some more. I cannot give words to what was taking place, but something new was being born in me. I wanted nothing of the outside world; all I wanted was to stay in His presence. You see, it is easy to go to church and lift your hands up in praise when all is well; but when your world has fallen apart, oh, what a sweet incense unto God when you get on your knees and praise Him anyway!

Though in the natural so much had been taken from me, I knew I served a supernatural, almighty God, and He was doing something great in my life. In all this, I had a deep yearning to pray in the Spirit. I felt a deep need to just keep praying. I did not know what exactly I was to pray for, but I stayed in His presence.

One day my church announced a special women's conference called "Waking Up the Lioness in You," with Joann Rosario Condrey[5]. I knew I needed to go, despite any obstacles that got in my way. Oh, my goodness! I was completely soaked in His presence, and that was just at the beginning of worship. About a half hour into worship, the speaker asked anyone who wanted to receive the baptism of the Holy Spirit to come to the altar. I could not get there fast enough. I could not stop crying; the love I was experiencing was like the love I experienced at the weekend retreat earlier in my life, but now in an even greater way. My crying out to God in English suddenly turned into something I was not aware of. It was amazing. I did not know what I was praying, but I knew the Holy Spirit in me knew. That was all I needed, because even though I did not know what exactly to pray for, the Holy Spirit did (Romans 8:26). I knew at this time I was baptized with the Holy Spirit. I am so thankful for that experience that has saved my life, my home, my children and the many others I have been called to pray for since.

This was the beginning of a whole new realm of the Spirit in my life. Two years passed by very quickly. When I look back at my life, it was like a bomb went off around me. Many people left my life except for a select few, and slowly God brought new people into my life who brought me closer to Him, as opposed to away from Him. I also noticed, because of the location He had me in, I was in hiding. The Lord needed to keep me away, out of sight, to eventually be out of mind of many people who had no good purpose in my life. His plans and purpose for my life were much greater than my limited thoughts for myself (Jeremiah 29:11-12). This amazing woman who opened the doors to her house and heart was the vessel God used. We grew close to each other. It was like a mother and daughter bond, because she had a daughter my age who hadn't spoken to her for the past seven years, and my own mother had passed away seven years before, so the whole relationship has been a blessing for both of us. She would always tell me that she didn't save me, I saved her by giving her a family.

How about you, my friend? Has there been a time when it looked like a spiritual bomb went off in your life, and though you did not see it at first, you later saw God's hand in every area in your life that needed cleaning? What were those areas? How do you feel now? We may not understand many things in our lives, but as long as we seek God's presence and guidance, we will be led to the better path for our lives.

NOTES

9

HELP FROM THE
HOLY GHOST
AT HOME

HELP FROM THE
HOLY GHOST AT HOME

Earthly wisdom is doing what comes naturally. Godly wisdom is doing what the Holy Spirit compels us to do.
Charles Stanley

After receiving the baptism of the Holy Spirit, or as older versions of Scripture call Him, the "Holy Ghost," I grew closer to God and hungrier for the things of God. I wanted to serve more inside the church, but understood my main ministry was in my home, my workplace, and the random places of life where I would talk to people. In this, I understood that if we are to be the hands and feet of Jesus, we need to be willing to go to other places, sometimes uncomfortable ones where we would not normally want to go.

It is important for us to recognize that God does not want His people serving just in church; we are needed in all arenas of life. We are needed in government, entertainment, schools, sports, and in any and every area we can think of. It might be a simple, small conversation of encouragement with the stressed-out cashier ringing up our items, or it might be a specific outreach to our communities. We really don't know what others are facing in their lives. Whether it be their hurt, loss, or pain, let us be mindful that they also are children of God. We do have to be careful, however, in reaching out to others, because we must make sure whatever we say aligns with Scripture and not our own beliefs. We do not want to misdirect any of God's children. To have the mind of Christ is to know that the possibilities are endless, and the closer our walk with God, the more sensitive we are to His calling. As Scripture says, "My sheep hear my voice…" (John 10:27).

Despite all the bad and fake news these days, an exciting movement of God is taking place. Holy Ghost revivals are going on, but unfortunately, they are more apparent in other countries than in America. Our country seems to give more attention to destroying the lives of others through gossip and hate, whether it is the rich and famous or the high school kids who think that they don't fit in because they are not as perfect as their classmates on social media. But oh, how beautiful it is to be a witness to the move of God, with His healing today just as powerful as in the Scriptures! People are being healed and demons cast out. Yes, my friend, you read right; people healed, and demons cast out. It is still happening today, because Jesus said if we believe in the works that He did, we will do them also, and will do even greater things than He did (John 14:12). The story with my younger daughter was scary. There were times when I felt I was being held back not to continue praying through the house. I would feel chills, discomfort and sudden fear, but greater was my fear of losing my home and kids and therefore I kept pushing through in prayer. That was when holy anger kicked in.

I recall one specific time I was praying around the house. Usually I would stop near the entrance of the girls' room. At the time they were much younger and sharing a room. But this specific day I realized that mess was a barrier for me not to enter their room and pray. I went right in and prayed in the center of the room, and interestingly enough, they themselves cleaned their room after that. No need to fight with our kids. They are having a hard time trying to figure out what is going on themselves. My daughter was about eight one day when she saw me and ran to her room. When I saw her, she was in tears. She said she knew she wanted to see me but felt something in her that wanted to hate me. She ran to her room and started crying because she said she loved me and never wanted to feel like that again towards me. If you're a parent, talk to your kids a lot because they need direction. Our kids today are more lost than ever but know that when we don't know what's really going on with them, rest assured because the Holy Ghost knows and will help you and your children in every area of their lives and yours. It is the best supernatural experience ever.

Many people today are fascinated with paranormal and supernatural activities seen in shows and movies. My youngest daughter and daughter-in-law are fascinated by it. I admit, I was too in my young teenage years. I could watch *The Exorcist* and other similar movies alone in the dark and not let it bother me. That was until I found out that many of these things are real. Many people do not realize the extent of the torture that other people experience, thinking they must continue to live that way if the problem is in them. Or if the problem is in the house, they assume they must move out. There is also the idea that only a Catholic priest can save such people, but what if there is no priest around to save them? What if the torturing spirit comes in the form of a friend, spouse, or other family member?

Well, my friend, do I have good news for you! There is a Spirit today who can guide you, protect you, give you wisdom, and empower you to rebuke and cast down those demonic strongholds that try to keep you limited or paralyzed in life. That Spirit is alive today, and just as powerful as when written about in Scripture in the book of Acts. That Spirit is the Holy Spirit of God. The situation with my daughter was a very challenging one, but praise God, today she is well.

One other example of the Holy Spirit's help that I have experienced personally was with my ex-husband. At this point in my life, I knew I had freedom in Christ. As I tell people, you may not have twenty-four-hour police protection, but you can have twenty-four-hour God protection. Anyway, one day my second husband at the time called me before coming home and was arguing with me on the phone. I did not know what he was mad about, but he was just angry in an odd way. When I got off the phone, I started praying, and suddenly I experienced what I call a "holy anger." I was reciting scriptures back to God and telling Him that before I did not know the Word and His benefits, but now I did. Satan was trying to work his way into my home, and that was unacceptable, I said. "I refuse to allow him into my safe haven," I declared, and then I told the Lord to do whatever needed to be done to keep out any demonic spirits.

Fast forward to my second husband driving up to the house. He stayed in his pickup for a few minutes, talking on his cell, and then he came in and sat down quietly. After about twenty minutes, I asked him if he was okay. He said he could not talk because when he had gotten out of the truck, he slammed the door on his thumb, and the pain would not permit him to talk.

Now you may say that was just a coincidence. Well, let me tell you of another time, when I was having the grand opening for the daycare. At that time, I did not understand my ex-husband's behavior, anger, and outbursts as much as I do today, but I did not want any of my visitors to feel uncomfortable as a result of his comments or remarks, so I prayed. I said to the Lord, "Lord, this daycare has received Your blessing today because I honor You and want all who enter to feel the comfort of Your presence. With the pastor, we will pray and bless this facility in Your name. Lord, all I ask is that You do not let that man say anything that would offend any of our guests. Please numb his tongue in the event that he does intend to say anything."

Well, shortly after the guests arrived, the facility was blessed, and we ate and celebrated. The man was quiet through the whole event. The only words he said were, "I'll meet you at home." I must admit, I was a little frightened, but I trusted God in this. When I got home, my ex-husband was lying down. He said he had hurt his back so badly he could not even talk.

One thing I need to make clear in all this is that I never wished him any harm. To this day, I do not wish him or anyone any harm, because I know if I hold any ill wishes toward him, it will only come back to me. But what a mighty God we serve, who makes sure we know not to be discouraged or afraid because the battle is not ours, but His (2 Chronicles 20:15). Our job is to forgive, though that is not always easy.

In forgiving and letting God be God, I was set free. Through the guidance of the Holy Spirit, I learned to keep my peace and forgive my ex-husband for many hurtful words he spoke out and my children heard as they also watched us through the window. Seven years later, we finally had a good friendship, similar to that of good friends or siblings. When people ask me how I managed

77

to be good friends with him after all we went through, I just smile and say, "Pray for your enemies."

Are you in a challenging situation where you find it hard to pray for that person who hurt you so badly? I know it is hard to let go, but it is not worth holding on to. I promise, if you seek help from God through His Holy Spirit, you can be free and healed from the spirit of heaviness.

Think about it: is holding on to a grudge and not forgiving someone worth missing out on heaven? Many people who have had a "heaven and hell" experience say that many people in hell are there mainly due to unforgiveness. Not all, but many of them. I would not want that for anyone. I know we all face many challenging people in our lives, and we all have many past hurts, but no one is worth going to hell for. Ask the Holy Spirit to help you with your unforgiveness and it shall be done because in the end no one is worth losing your salvation over.

NOTES

10

JESUS IN THE PARK IN OUR HOMES, AND EVERYWHERE

JESUS IN THE PARK, IN OUR HOMES, AND EVERYWHERE

We must accept finite disappointment, but we must never lose infinite hope.

Dr. Martin Luther King, Jr.

I have a dear pastor friend who partners with a few other churches to minister in the heart of town in the ghetto area. Every third week, they go to the park with a karaoke machine to worship, and to feed and minister to the homeless. My children and I had the privilege to help feed some of these people, and we saw a very powerful move of God. These people were broken, but too ashamed to step foot into a church because of their failures, hurts, and disappointments. They had lost hope in themselves and in the world. This is a strategy of the enemy. He watches to see when your guard is down, because he knows that to move in on you, he must weaken you first through fear, defeat, and rejection.

Some of the volunteers in the park were serving because they themselves had been in those shoes and wanted to share the hope they found in Jesus. They were able to get out of their mess, seek help, and find life again, so they felt the need to help others find Jesus. You could see and feel a true move of God in that park. It was sad yet beautiful to see people who were broken, lost, and discouraged sing, worship, and praise God in ways that I do not see many in church do.

I think they dim the lights in church so that you cannot really see around you. When you look at some people, it is as if their lips are so tightly sealed, they cannot get their words out to sing. Or their arms are glued so tightly to their sides they cannot raise them in surrender. I remember growing up in my church and seeing people who looked like they had been baptized in vinegar. That was always puzzling to me, because I always thought you would want to come to church to be refreshed with the Word.

So, seeing all this praise and worship taking place in an open area was amazing. After the outreach finished, we heard stories leading to hope and happy new beginnings. I remember one specific guy who pointed at a bench and told us that he was saved on that bench and gave his life to Jesus. Glory be to God! Unfortunately, this was not the case for all, because some people let their situations become so much a part of their lives that they cannot even see there is a problem. We can do our part, but if they are not willing to receive it, there is nothing we can do.

Sadly, it is the same for many people who are used to complaining, hating, being unforgiving, gossiping, feeling sick, etc. They have allowed those things to become such a great part of them that they do not see a need to fix anything. They say things like, "That's just the way I am," or "I don't know how else to be." Because they are so stuck in their ways, it's very difficult, if not impossible, to get them to believe there is a better way that can also lead to better spiritual health.

The pessimism is so strong sometimes that it exhausts you. Even though you try to help, nothing can convince them that they can do certain things to improve their lives, even if they are only baby steps. This puts in perspective what the Bible means when it says, "Because of their unbelief, He could not do many miracles." (Matthew 13:58).

In my years of helping people in and out of the medical field, I have seen some people with amazing determination to make life better, while others are not ready to change. Basically, we should just pray for those who are not ready to change because we do not want to force our help onto those who do not want to receive it. We must keep in mind that our timing is not their timing, and in pushing them, we risk creating bitterness in them. I have learned to just go behind the scenes and pray for them, lifting them up to God, being careful to pray for God's will and not my own.

To pray for our will rather than God's is manipulative, controlling prayer designed to work for our benefit and not for the other person's. I know it can hurt, especially when a child of ours or someone we care deeply for is on the wrong path. But maybe that is the path they need to walk to get to where they need to be. As they go through their troubles in life, they may eventually be able to help others because of their own personal experiences, just as I have been able to help others because of my past experiences.

Furthermore, any spoken words may need to come from someone else and not from you specifically. It's like listening to certain preachers; they all may be saying the same thing, bringing the same message, but different people receive it better from one than the other.

I recall a very special person I deeply care for. She loves the Lord, but her approach, I feel, is more of a reprimand rather than one of comfort. I know she means well, but she appears to be open only to her own perspective.

Then you have situations like that of an angry and upset spouse who wants to run away with the kids to hurt the other parent. The one parent knows that if she confronts him, he will blow up because he is already angry and not thinking straight. You hear so many crazy things in the news that it is easy to be tempted to let fear take over, but this is when she must go to the throne instead of the phone. She must pray for God to send someone to help him think before he does something outrageous that might jeopardize the children and his relationship with them.

Sure enough, a well-known family friend sees him. As the father vents and shares his idea of taking the kids to hurt the mother, the friend asks him, "Who do you think will really get hurt in this situation?" The father stops to think and tells him, "The kids will be the ones hurt the most." That simple God-sent conversation changes the outcome of what could have been a disaster.

Have you ever found yourself in a situation where you knew your voice was not the voice that needed to be heard to change a specific situation, and then here comes someone else who very smoothly got the point across? That is okay, because our words, voice, and message are not for everybody. Don't allow yourself to be discouraged just because some people, especially someone close to you, does not accept your message. There will always be some random person that will need to hear what you have to say, and it may even save their lives.

NOTES

11

Do We Want Help or Do We Just Like Talking About our Problems

DO WE WANT HELP, OR
DO WE JUST LIKE TALKING
ABOUT OUR PROBLEMS?

But seek first the kingdom of God and His righteousness, and all these things will be added to you.

Matthew 6:33

I once heard a little phrase that will stay with me forever. I share it with as many people as I can, whenever they find themselves facing a challenge. It's short, simple, sweet, and oh so powerful, the phrase is, "*Before you go to the phone, go to The Throne*." To this day, I find this phrase helpful because God Himself provides the resources and people to help in any situation, no matter what it is.

How many problems, or "challenges," as I like to refer to them, could have been better solved if, instead of calling everyone we could think of to vent and complain, we would have just brought them to the throne of grace? I mean, think about it. How much energy has gone into telling people your problems—problems they can't help you with and, worse, may give you advice about that makes your situation worse than it was to begin with?

It never ceases to amaze me when I see the way people throw their problems out there to just about anybody, as if there is nothing to it. They share information with people who have not earned the right to know their personal business. Do not get me wrong; it is good to share our testimony, and sometimes we may feel we can help others by sharing certain situations from our lives. However, we need to be very careful that we are speaking life to the good things, not giving more life to what is not so good in our lives.

I honestly feel bad when I see people talking about their problems, week after week. Deep inside, it is a cry for help, but their pride or confusion in the situation does not allow them to come to terms with their needs. You must be careful when speaking to such people, and you must choose your words well before you become the one ruining their bashing moment. I mean, don't get me wrong. It's okay to have a one-day pity party and vent, but then let it go.

You also don't want to talk about other people who are not there to defend themselves. That is gossip, and the Bible is very clear in letting us know we are not to gossip about anyone (see James 1:26; Proverbs 10:18–19; and many other verses in the Bible). There are curses attached to gossip.

There might also be a scary situation ahead of you, and you are tempted to speak of the worst-case scenario instead of the better one. Unfortunately, many of us have been taught to always picture the worst-case scenario instead of the better one. This is very discouraging, because if done frequently, it can make you lose hope in the good things and only expect the worst. I have a few friends whom I love dearly, but I feel bad for them because they are stuck in their ways, and do not wait for anyone to listen to them; they speak it to themselves. I'm sure you heard random people mumbling to themselves, calling themselves names, not realizing what they are say is prophesying those lies over themselves.

If you are talking weeks and months later about the same thing happening in your life, most likely there is a deep hurt attached to it, and that's okay. We've all been through hurts, some more than others, but we've all had our share. I am not making light of anyone's situation, because I have been in or have been there for others in very challenging situations that can break us badly. When I'm going through challenges, however, I now make it my business to go on my knees in prayer. No time to waste, that's for sure.

Whatever the situation I'm facing at the moment, I know my Father in heaven will help me get through it. It may not seem like it sometimes, but I repeat to myself, *"This too shall pass*, and *Help is on the way."* You see, our Father in heaven promised to never leave us or forsake us (Hebrews 13:5, Deuteronomy 31:6 and 31:8). After we come humbly to Him, we must learn to trust in Him and His ways, because they are sometimes very far from what we would expect. We must always learn to seek Him in all things and trust in Him.

Just this past week, my sixteen-year-old daughter took her first flight alone to spend time with her father for the summer in Puerto Rico. Well, as my child parted from me and went to her gate, I noticed the flight was delayed half an hour. *"No big deal"*, I thought at first, since we had just had a recent thunderstorm. I was in contact with her and she was fine. She told me she was waiting to get on board, and she did board the plane, but then they were told to get back off. This went on, back and forth, for several hours because of the storm.

In my heart, I felt tempted to speak the worst-case scenario, but I did not want to give life to the thoughts that ran through my mind, because as Scripture says, "Death and life are in the power of the tongue" (Proverbs 18:21). I refused to speak any negative words into the situation. What I did instead was to praise, with some tears, my Father in heaven and ask Him to please take care of my baby, who was growing up to be a mighty woman of God. I tell you, I felt Him in my heart, saying, *"Trust Me. I'm doing something here."*

My child's flight was delayed five hours, and she finally arrived safely in Puerto Rico at 1:30 a.m. When I read the newspaper the next day, I saw thousands of people in protest covering the highways of San Juan on the day and at the time she was originally scheduled to arrive. I couldn't help but burst into tears at work, letting everyone know how God had kept my daughter from being caught in the middle of that protest. She got there when the streets were clean, and everyone was cleared out of the way. God used a storm in New Jersey to keep my baby girl safe from protest in Puerto Rico demanding the governor to resign[6]. Glory be to God!

What about the situations when someone has a sick bone in their body, but there is someone else who always has more sick bones in their body? These people are the ones who feel they need to be sicker and taking more medications than the person they are talking to. If one has one issue, the other has more issues with more medications, as if magnifying their problem makes their situation better.

This part hits home to me, coming from the medical field. I am still left speechless when I hear the conversations of people who started with one medication but are now taking other medications to fix the side effects from the first medication, and still have not gotten to the root of their problem. Don't get me wrong, I know there are many good doctors out there who really care and want to help their patients, but I also know there are patients who want to get fixed without putting their own effort into it. I have had plenty of those. Those are difficult patients to help, because you really can't help those who don't want to help themselves.

In my many years of experience, I have concluded that it is imperative that we be physically healthy as well as mentally and spiritually healthy. I believe they go hand in hand. If you take care of yourself physically, you have a better chance to recoup more quickly from a needed medical procedure. If you are mentally and spiritually healthy, you are better prepared when life throws the unexpected at you.

I thank God for discernment in hearing a certain sermon at a certain time that gave me a message I needed at that time. I love my church, but I recognize there are times I needed more during the week besides just reading The Word. Pastor John Hagee has given me the courage to take the authority given to me over my children.[8] I wish one day I could meet Bishop T. D. Jakes and give him a great big hug because he has helped me to recognize how my thinking differently was God's gift to me. There have been many times his messages have left me sobbing like a baby and all I could say in the midst of my tears was, "He understands me!"[9]

When I went through a great loss, I had people calling me, some of whom were religious leaders, telling me they were worried about me. They could not understand how I was so peaceful after having lost so much. I truly had a peace that surpasses all understanding, and I reminded them that my Father in heaven promised to never leave me or forsake me. I told them I was holding on to His promises and praising Him in my situation.

Then there were the patients I knew on a personal level who had given me their whole line of troubles and medications. Because I knew them personally, I was comfortable with them and I often asked them if they had prayed about their problem before seeking medical attention, asking God to direct them in what they needed and to provide the right doctor, diagnosis, and medications. Some gave me a puzzled look, like that was a trick question. Others just wanted to zap me away with their dark looks. And some were humble enough to say they had never thought of that. For those of you who may not have thought of that, I can't emphasize enough the need to pray for direction and the proper help.

I can tell you of many stories where I planned my day from beginning to end, yet the Lord took me down another path, just as Proverbs 16:9 says. Sometimes my patients themselves have said that I was the answer to their prayer. I remember one time I had just gotten home from work at about 11:30 p.m., when I got a call to go see another patient in an area that was not normally mine. As tired as I was, I felt in my heart that I needed to go. When I arrived, before I even introduced myself, the man looked at me and said, "You are the one I prayed for." I took care of him as best as I could, holding my tears back, comforting him, and glad that I was obedient to the prompting of the Holy Spirit in taking that hour drive to see him.

How about you, my friend? Do you seek help and guidance from the Holy Spirit in your situation or from that of a loved one, or anyone who may listen to you? Be careful who you allow access into your personal life. A person should earn the right to know your personal business.

NOTES

12

FINDING GOD
IN QUIETNESS

FINDING GOD IN QUIETNESS

Be still and know that I am God.
Psalm 4:10

In such a time as we are living in today, it is imperative to seek God's presence and guidance. He longs to fellowship with humanity, to abide in us as we abide in Him. When Jesus taught us how to talk to the Father in the example known as the Lord's Prayer (Matthew 6:9–13), the intent wasn't for us to recite it several times a day; rather, it was an example of how to speak to God. Unfortunately, some of the newer versions of the Bible have omitted the end part of the prayer, and just placing it as a foot note so tiny at bottom of the page, "For Yours is the kingdom, the power, and the glory, forever. Amen." I don't understand why something so important would be left out, but it has. It is however, found in the King James version. I believe now more than ever; we need to seek Him while He may be found (Isaiah 55:6).

There may be times when we ramble on and on to our Father in heaven about our challenges (I don't like to call them problems). We can go on and on, but we can't expect to hear anything if we don't take the time to be quiet. There is something to giving ourselves a quiet time with our Father in heaven, whether first thing in the morning or late at night before bed. Does it have to be in the morning or at night? No, it does not, but it definitely has to be time purposely set aside for Him. This helps us renew and recoup. It is also good, when we are pouring out our hearts with what I call the "ugly cry," or wailing, to give ourselves a little quiet time to find peace, seek guidance, or actually hear a word from the Lord.

One day I was upset and crying out to God about a house I was trying to buy. I cannot explain how, but I knew in my heart this house was for me. It was a ranch-style house, which was good because I was thinking long term, not wanting to go up and down stairs as I got older. There were other houses close by, but not too close. I loved the location because the house was somewhat tucked away but close enough to shopping centers.

I was running around to get all the paperwork needed for the loan and closing, but every time I turned around, it seemed they needed something else. Then, out of the blue, they wanted a cosigner. In my weariness, I cried out to God and said, "Lord, is this house for me? I'm tired of trying and doing. If this house is not for me, please tell me and I will stop, or give me a sign and I will get my fight back up and keep going." Sure enough, as I stayed quiet but remaining in His presence, I heard as clear as day, "Who has the last say?" I smiled and said, "You, Lord, have the last say." Then I realized not only does He have the last He has the only say, everything else is there to have us lose focus in Him and His word.

From this I received supernatural energy and got my fight back. This word from the Lord was confirmed by someone sending me a song on my phone that had some lyrics saying, "When Jesus says yes, nobody can say no." I remember saying to God, "I will keep going because I know You are with me. Jesus, I need You to be my co-signer because I will not go in without You, and no one else will be on that deed." Long story short, I got my home with only my signature because Jesus was my be-hind-the-scenes cosigner. To God be the glory!

Jesus Himself recognized the need for a quiet time, often getting away from it all. We all need that, but not everyone seeks it. We must implement the advice of my school counselor and tell our loved ones they need to be respectful of our time, especially of our quiet time with Jesus. Think about the many times you wake up around two or three in the morning. Maybe it isn't so much insomnia as it is our heavenly Father wanting quiet intimacy with you at a time when there are no distractions.

Another idea for a quiet time, if you work, use your break time as a quiet time for yourself instead of hanging around with the gossipers and complaining along with everyone else. Complaining only drains your energy, because when you complain, you are magnifying your situation and giving access to the enemy, thereby minimizing what God can do. Furthermore, when you are having your quiet time, do not dwell on the things you need to do or the mistakes of the past that you can't change. If that happens, stop and think where you are now, and move forward.

In silence, not only can we hear better from God and enjoy a spiritual renewal, but we also benefit by curbing the temptation to speak something negative. To this day, many people do not realize the power and weight of their words. As mentioned in Proverbs 18:21, life and death are in the power of the tongue. The more time passes, the more I see that a person at work can destroy their department, a parent can destroy their home, and a medical patient can experience defeat because of the words they speak. Many people have spoken doubt to great opportunities and then complained about the failure they themselves helped manifest. I believe that's why Joshua led the people in silence (Joshua 6). If they had spoken one word, it might have been a complaint; and in their complaining, they would not have obtained the victory the Lord had for them in tearing down the walls.

Then you have the book of Luke, chapter 1, when the angel Gabriel spoke with Zacharias, letting him know he was going to be a father. His wife, Elizabeth, was going to have a son, but the words that came out of his mouth were words of doubt. Because of Zacharias's doubt, the angel rendered him silent until the baby was born. Finally, as they prepared for John's circumcision on the eighth day after birth, Zacharias was finally able to speak, and he praised the Lord. Could you imagine not being able to speak for almost a year, being forced into silence?

Coming from the medical field myself, I love the movie *"Breakthrough[7]"*. I know firsthand of medical staff who have been on the job a little too long or who just refuse to accept that our Lord is still alive and doing miracles as He did back in the days of Scripture. They tend to show more faith in medicine than in the God who created it all. When I was young in the field, a little over twenty years ago, I remember a psychiatrist telling me that people don't get it. They don't get that medicine can take them only so far, but the will to live can do what no medicine can. That, together with prayer and faith, can really work miracles.

I believe that in both the biblical cases I mentioned above, people were not allowed to speak so that their words would not contradict God's will. I know there are times when we do need to speak up, but that is a whole different topic in itself.

Can you think of a time when you realized your silent time with God brought you to a much-needed renewal in your life? How did it change you? The time with our heavenly Father can be better than any therapy or medicine we can take because He can get right to the root of the issue and make us new. People will start noticing you look different and at peace.

NOTES

FINAL WORDS

In closing, I would like to add a few words. I do not claim in any way, shape, or form to be a high-ranking scholar. I am, however, bringing an overall experience of the God of the Bible, the true living and true loving God who wants to fellowship with the humanity He created. Despite our many imperfections, He loves us with a love that we cannot begin to fathom. He does not want us to live in bondage to the enemy but to have freedom that is found only in the Father, Son and the Holy Spirit.

I don't know about you, but it surely gives me peace of mind knowing that even though we live in this cold, cruel world, there is a Father in heaven who loves us beyond comprehension. In fact, He loved us so much that He sent His only begotten Son to heal, deliver, and save us. According to John 3:16–17, whosoever believes in Him shall not perish but have eternal life. This passage goes on to say that, "He did not come to condemn the world, but to save it."

Jesus taught us to be alert and not just let life happen to us. To have the mind of Christ is a deep knowing that we are in this world but not of it. We need to put on the full armor of God (Ephesians 6:11–12) so as not to be deceived into thinking that the salvation of our precious soul is from anything the world teaches or invents. What the world teaches can many times bring more confusion. According to scripture, salvation does not come from saints, sorcery, aliens, bracelets, charms or angels. Salvation comes from Jesus Christ, our Lord and Savior, and according to Romans 8:38–39, nothing can separate us from the love of God that is in Christ Jesus our Lord.

My friend, we are living in very challenging times today. Everything is being challenged, from our faith to our culture. I feel deep in my being, that just like in the time of Noah, God is calling us to repentance. He wants us to experience a radical change of mind and heart so that we come to Him and find Him while He may still be found. There won't be an ark like in Noah's time, but in my mind, I see doors slamming shut and I hear people screaming and crying for help, but it will be too late. Like God, I do not want anyone to be left behind, but it is obvious that time is definitely running out.

The good news is that there is hope and you have a chance for salvation. According to Romans 10:9–11, "If you confess with your mouth, 'Jesus is Lord,' and believe in your heart that God raised Him from the dead, you will be saved. For it is with your heart that you believe and are justified, and it is with your mouth that you confess and are saved." Anyone who trusts in Him will never be put to shame." I pray you take the opportunity to know God at a deeper lever and accept Jesus as your Lord and Savior, because we are not promised tomorrow.

God Bless,

L. B. Rodriguez

ENDNOTES

1. Dear Abby was an advice columnist. Her real name was Pauline Friedman Phillips (1918-2013) Her legend is continued by her daughter Jeanne Phillips. Google - Times of Israel

2. Catherine Ponder is an American Minister and author. One of the world's leading prosperity writers. Her first prosperity book "The Dynamic Laws of Prosperity" first published in the early 1960's. CatherinePonder.www.hubs.com

3. Evangelist John Ramirez is a former high-ranking satanic priest from New York, that now serves The Lord, helping set the captives free as he brings the message of deliverance that is found in Christ. John Ramirez Ministries

4. Derek Prince (1915-2003) Was born in India of British parents. He was an international Bible teacher. He was probably most noted for his teachings about deliverance from demonic oppression and about Israel - MGMMinistries.org, Derek Prince Ministries

5. Joan Rosario Condrey is an American Gospel singer and is Senior Pastor with her husband Cory Condrey in Rain Fire Church, Douglasville, Georgia

6. Puerto Rico protest in the streets of San Juan- New York Times July 23,2019

7. Pastor John Hagee - John Charles Hagee (born April 12, 1940) is the founder and senior pastor of Cornerstone Church in San Antonio, Texas, a non-denominational charismatic church with more than 19,000 active members. John Hagee is CEO at his non-profit corporation, Global Evangelism Television (GETV).

8. Bishop T. D. Jakes - Thomas Dexter Jakes Sr. (born June 9, 1957), known as T. D. Jakes, is a pastor, author and filmmaker. He is the pastor of The Potter's House, a non-denominational American megachurch. Bishop Jakes's church services and evangelistic sermons are broadcast on The Potter's Touch, which airs on Lightsource.com, the Trinity Broadcasting Network, Black Entertainment Television, the Daystar Television Network and The Word Network.

9. Breakthrough - 2019 film based on a true story from 20th Century Fox, Directed by Roxanne Dawson and Produced by Devon Franklin. Stephen Curry and Rev. Dr. Samuel Rodriguez were the Executive Producers. Story written by Joyce Smith

-----

Made in the USA
Middletown, DE
08 October 2022